Ocean Freighter Heyday

Malcolm Cranfield

Federal Steam Navigation's ***Middlesex*** was built at the Glasgow yard of Alexander Stephen & Sons in 1953. We see her near Montreal in June 1965. She had sailed from Lyttelton on 25 March 1965, passing through the Panama Canal on 15 May. In 1968 she was transferred within the P&O Group to British India S. N. Co. and renamed ***Jelunga***. From 1972 largely trading between Australasia and the Persian Gulf, in 1975 she was absorbed into the P&O Strath Services fleet as ***Strathleven*** and was beached for breaking at Gadani Beach, Pakistan, on 8 November 1977.

(Simon Olsen collection)

Introduction

The three decades following the end of the Second World War, before the container revolution took hold over dry cargo shipping, may be described as the "Ocean Freighter Heyday". Many ships which survived the War remained in service well into the 1960s while newly-built ships were only slowly developed from pre-war designs. This book looks at British and north Continental European ships which were serving international trade until the end of the 1970s.

The four sections of the book cover some of the best known companies offering scheduled cargo liner services plus views of ships berthed in the U.K. and north continental ports, with a few overseas, and of ships underway in local rivers and waterways. A final section looks at tramp ships. These older and slower vessels had mainly voyaged worldwide carrying bagged, neo-bulk or bulk cargoes although many found employment on charter to cargo liner companies.

Acknowledgements

Many thanks are extended to Simon Olsen, Paul Boot and Harry Stott for their immense help in providing photographs from their collections and for helping with the captions. Grateful thanks are also extended to other friends who have kindly allowed the use of their photographs, notably Dr. George Wilson of Blackburn, who had served with the Ocean Group and the R.F.A. and is custodian of the slides taken by his late brother Geoffrey, a radio officer with B.P., and also Alan Lee on behalf of the late Norman Hesketh, Andrew Wiltshire on behalf of his late father John, my cousin John D. Hill, custodian of the late Richard Parsons' collection, Malcolm Donnelly, Alastair Paterson, Dave Salisbury, Douglas Cromby, Peter Fitzpatrick,

Gerhard Fiebiger and Karl-Josef Hagenkötter of Germany, Trevor Jones and Ian Shiffman of South Africa, Russell Priest from Australia and René Beauchamp from Canada. All photographs which are not my own are reproduced with their permission and, where known, of the original photographer. Thanks are also due to Nigel Jones, Jim Prentice, Bertil Palm of Sweden and Risto Brzoza of Finland for their help with captions. I am grateful to Gil Mayes for his diligent proof reading and to Gomer Press for their excellent printing.

Malcolm Cranfield   Portishead and Heswall   September 2020

Front cover: The *Barrister* of the Charente S. S. Co. Ltd. (Harrison Line) was built in 1954 at the Doxford shipyard in Sunderland. She was photographed as she departed from Cape Town in March 1973 during a voyage from Lourenço Marques (now Maputo) to Glasgow and Manchester. In September 1974 she was sold at Manchester to Roussos Bros., of Piraeus, and renamed *George*. Although not broken up until 1984, she had been laid up at Piraeus as *Georgy* from February 1977. Harrison Line dated from 1853 when the brothers Thomas and James Harrison took control of the shipping and shipbroking interests of George Brown and Harrison. Starting business with brigs engaged in the wine trade, small steamers named *Cognac* and *Gladiator* were built in 1860 for their Charente Steamship Company to cater for the expanding trade in brandy shipments from France. Charente's first iron ship, named *Philosopher*, delivered in 1857 to trade to India, had established the standard naming theme of trades or professions. Over the years Charente's services were extended to the Caribbean and U.S. Gulf, East and South Africa. The line's last vessel, the chartered *Barrister*, built in 1994, became *P&O Nedlloyd Kilindini*.

(Ian Shiffman, Malcolm Cranfield collection)

Back cover: The Manchester Ship Canal has certain advantages and disadvantages for ship photography, favourite spots being where the canal has a wider stretch such as at Ellesmere Port, east of the docks, and at Runcorn beyond the rail and road bridges which can clearly be seen in this photograph. During the era of general cargo ships it was often necessary to de-mast inward ships at the crane berth in Eastham. Funnel tops were taken off and landed on the quay while top masts, radar masts and heavy lift derricks were lowered, all in order to allow passage up the canal to Salford docks. In this photograph the *Ebro* of Royal Mail Lines, built by Harland & Wolff at Govan in 1952, is seen passing Runcorn after being prepared in that way for the passage to Manchester. Fortunately her funnel was low enough not to require surgery. Launched as *Tuscany*, she instead served Royal Mail as *Ebro* until sold early in 1969 to Fortunewind Maritime Ltd of Hong Kong and renamed *Fortune Victory*. In mid-1970 she was resold to the Union of Burma Five Star Line, taking the name *Kalemyo*, as which she arrived at Tsingtao for breaking in December 1978.

(Eddie Jackson, Simon Olsen collection)

Cunard Steamship Co. Ltd.'s **Alaunia**, the third ship given the name, was built at Port Glasgow in 1960 at Wm. Hamilton's Glen Yard. She is seen passing Erith in the River Thames, inbound from New York for London's Royal Docks, in May 1969. As Cunard had recently joined the Atlantic Container Line consortium, whose containers can be seen on deck, **Alaunia** was soon redundant on North Atlantic services. Founded in 1840 as the British and North American Royal Mail Steam Packet Company, by the 1880s fast ships were plying between Liverpool and New York; routes to other countries were later added. In 1934 Cunard was merged with White Star Line, forming Cunard-White Star Limited, reverting to Cunard Steamship in 1949. From 1970 Cunard began to concentrate on cruising while diversifying its cargo operations to include reefer ships, tankers and bulk carriers. **Alaunia** was in that year transferred to Brocklebank services and renamed **Malancha**. Sold in May 1971 together with sistership **Macharda** (ex **Andania**) to Far East based buyers, becoming **Humi Nasita** and **Humi Mahis**, a resale to China in 1973 saw her briefly employed internationally as **Yungming** and then locally as **Hong Qi 108** until broken up in the late 1980s.

(Simon Olsen collection)

Our first section looks at the ships of some of the well-known shipping lines. Scottish Shire Line Ltd's *Argyllshire* was built at Greenock in 1956. We see her outbound from Durban early one morning during January 1974. She had sailed from Liverpool on 12 December 1973 for Beira. The name Scottish Shire Line was first used in 1893 by Turnbull, Martin & Company for services to New Zealand via South Africa and Australian ports. A joint Federal-Houlder-Shire Line was formed in 1904 and Cayzer, Irvine & Co Ltd. (Clan Line) acquired a controlling interest in Shire Line in 1910. From 1918 the Shire Line operated as part of Clan Line, although its ships retained their own naming system and yellow painted funnels until 1930. Transfers of vessels between the companies were commonplace, for example the first *Argyllshire*, built at Clydebank in 1911, was renamed *Clan Urquhart* in 1932 while this second *Argyllshire* was registered in the name of Clan Line until 1960. Sold in East Africa during the autumn of 1975 together with *Kinnaird Castle* (renamed *Nazeer*) to Monnoo Overseas Ltd of Dubai, as *Schivago* she returned to London for Clan Line before trading between Europe and India until broken up in Pakistan in August 1977. Her sistership *Ayrshire* was wrecked in March 1965 on the island of Abd-al-Kuri, part of the Socotra Archipelago, during a voyage from Liverpool to Sydney.

(Trevor Jones)

4

The **Bellerophon** of Ocean S.S. Co. Ltd. (Blue Funnel Line), seen at Hong Kong, was built at Dundee in 1950 in order to operate a service which could compete with the fastest sailing ships in the China trade, in 1866 Alfred and Philip Holt of Liverpool had taken delivery from Scott & Co. of Greenock of three new steamships, establishing the Ocean Steam Ship Company. Managed by Alfred Holt & Co. as the Blue Funnel Line, it became the best known shipping line in the trade. In 1902 China Mutual Steam Navigation Company, together with its fleet of steamers and services between China and the west coast of North America, was acquired followed in 1935 by Glen & Shire Lines after the Kylsant crash. Transfers of vessels between these companies were commonplace. For example **Bellerophon** was owned by Glen Line between 1957 and 1972 as **Cardiganshire** and from 1973 until her sale in 1976 was nominally owned by China Mutual. However she operated with a yellow funnel on Elder Dempster services to West Africa for much of 1975 before sailing to Jeddah in December 1975 on a joint service with local agents S. H. Alatas by whom the **Polydorus** (ex **Alcinous**) was briefly owned in 1976 as **Johara**. In mid-1976, together with sistership **Ascanius** (renamed **Mastura**) and following brief employment in a film as **Belle**, Orri Navigation of Jeddah had purchased **Bellerophon**, trading her as **Obhor**. Both ships were sold for breaking in 1978. Following the creation in 1967 of Overseas Containers, Blue Funnel Line's conventional services were gradually reduced, ending by 1978.

(Alastair Paterson collection, courtesy of Paul Boot)

Elder Dempster's' **Tamele** was built in 1945 by Cammell Laird at Birkenhead and was photographed by the ship's surgeon at Victoria (now Limbe), Cameroon, having sailed from Liverpool on 1 September 1965. Returning on 18 October, she continued trading between Liverpool and West Africa until early 1967. Sailing from Antwerp on 1 April 1967 for Shanghai under the new ownership of Guan Guan Shipping of Singapore, she was renamed **Golden City** in the Far East. She finally arrived at Hong Kong for breaking on 6 April 1973. In 1879 Alfred Jones had joined Alexander Elder and John Dempster, Liverpool agents for British & African S.N. Company, proceeding to create Elder Dempster Shipping Limited in 1899. Following Alfred Jones' death in 1909, the company's interests were purchased by Sir Owen Philipps (Lord Kylsant) whose Royal Mail Group collapsed in 1931. Elder Dempster was then managed until 1944 by Alfred Holt's Ocean Steamship Company and in 1965 became wholly owned by Ocean which subsequently invested in semi-container ships for the West African trade but withdrew from shipping in 1989, selling Elder Dempster to Delmas-Vieljeux which later became part of CMA CGM – the French Line.

(George Wilson)

The **Daru** of Guinea Gulf Line was built at the Greenock shipyard of Scotts' Shipbuilding and Engineering Company in 1958. We see her near Montréal in October 1971. She had arrived at Ashtabula (Ohio) on Lake Erie on 11 October from Sapele and departed from Detroit on 15 October bound for Douala. Built for Elder Dempster Lines, she had operated on Henderson Line's service to Burma as **Yoma** from November 1965 until early 1967. Then reverting to West African services, she was renamed **Daru** at Tilbury in August 1967 and soon thereafter transferred to Guinea Gulf Line. At some point before her sale at Tilbury to Sharjah-based interests in April 1979, **Daru** had reverted to Elder Dempster colours and retained a yellow funnel until the end. Initially renamed **Lone Eagle**, at the end of 1980 she took the name **Anjo One** but was idle at Karachi from February 1982 until sent to Gadani Beach for breaking, being beached on 8 September 1982.

(Al Sagon-King)

Glengarry arrives at London's Royal Docks in June 1969, having sailed from Hamburg on 27 May 1969 bound for Hsinkang via London and Cape Town. Built by Burmeister & Wain at Copenhagen, she was launched on 6 November 1939 and was being fitted out when German forces invaded Denmark on 9 April 1940. In November 1940 she was commissioned into the Kriegsmarine and renamed *Meersburg*. In April 1941 she was sent to Rotterdam for intended conversion into the raider *Hansa*. Two years later she was moved to Hamburg for the installation of secret equipment but instead, in February 1944, was commissioned as an artillery cadet training ship. In August 1944 she participated in the evacuation of refugees from Reval (Tallinn) and in May 1945 of troops from the Hela (Hél) Peninsula near Danzig (Gdańsk) to Lübeck Bay. Although sustaining damage when hitting a mine on 4 May 1945, she made her way to Kiel where she was taken as a prize by the Allies and returned to British ownership at Methil. Renamed *Empire Humber*, she was sent to Rotterdam for intended conversion to a Combined Operations HQ ship in the Pacific. However, when Japan surrendered she was still at Southampton and Glen Line sent the ship, in breach of an Admiralty Marshal's writ, to Gareloch on the Clyde, soon reverting to the name *Glengarry*. In mid-1970 she was transferred within the Ocean Group to Blue Funnel Line and renamed *Dardanus* but early in 1971 reverted in the Far East to her original name and was sold for breaking at Tadotsu, Japan. Alan Gow's Glen Line had entered the China tea trade using steamships following the opening of the Suez Canal in 1869. Glen Line Ltd, formed in 1910, was soon acquired by Elder Dempster and in 1920 amalgamated with the Shire Line, founded by David James Jenkins in 1860. In 1935, following the Kylsant crash, Glen & Shire Lines were taken over by Alfred Holt's Ocean Steamship Company.

(Simon Olsen collection)

The **Birmingham City** was built in 1946 at the Readhead shipyard in South Shields as **Baskerville** for Barberry's S. S. Co Ltd. (Runciman London Ltd), specialists in the carriage of newsprint. She was purchased in 1950 by the Bristol City Line of Steamships and photographed in the St. Lawrence River at Montréal in 1963. **Birmingham City** subsequently sailed from Avonmouth for the Far East on 23 August 1963 as **Semporna Bay**, becoming **Victoria Bay** in 1965 and arriving at Hong Kong on 10 August 1969 to be broken up. Bristol City Line was part of a company with shipbuilding and ship repairing interests which was founded in 1879 by Charles Hill who had taken over the business from George Hillhouse in 1845. Bristol City Line initially traded to the east coast of the USA, starting a service to Canada in 1933 which was extended to the Great Lakes in 1958. In 1971 Bristol City Line, which had the containership **Dart Atlantic** building at Hebburn-on-Tyne, was taken over by Bibby Line. In 1958 the ships owned by Barberry's S. S. Co Ltd, including a new **Baskerville**, built in 1954, were transferred to a new company named Transatlantic Carriers Ltd.

(Al Sagon King, courtesy of Ian Shiffman)

The **Cannanore** of the Peninsular and Oriental Steam Navigation Company (P&O) was berthed at L Shed in Avonmouth's Old Dock on 15 November 1970 discharging cargo from India. She had been built by Barclay, Curle & Co. at Whiteinch, Glasgow, and delivered on 5 July 1949. Sold at Singapore in February 1972 to Pac-Trade Nav. Co. (Madrigal Shipping Co. Inc. of Manila), she briefly traded to the Persian Gulf as **Santa Ana** before sailing from Manila on 20 August 1972 bound for Kaohsiung to be broken up. P&O was incorporated in 1840 when a contract was secured to deliver mail to Alexandria in Egypt. In 1969, together with Ocean Steamship (Blue Funnel Line), Furness Withy and British & Commonwealth, P&O had established Overseas Containers Limited (OCL) and in 1971 formed a General Cargo Division to operate the residual conventional fleets. However, by the early 1980s, all of P&O's former cargo liner routes had become container operations.

(Malcolm Cranfield)

The **Nuddea** was built for British India S. N. Co by Barclay Curle at Whiteinch in 1954. On 9 September 1963 she was photographed at Trincomalee, Ceylon (Sri Lanka), from Blue Funnel Line's **Memnon** which was on a voyage from Manila to Avonmouth. **Nuddea** subsequently sailed from Chittagong on 25 September 1963 bound for London while sistership **Nardana** would soon start a first voyage from London to Brisbane in P&O direct ownership as **Baradine**. Her reversion to British India ownership with new name of **Nardana** in 1968 lasted until 1972 when she became a unit of P&O's General Cargo Division before a sale in 1973 to Iran. As **Arya Pand** she was broken up in 1976. **Nuddea** however continued in British India ownership until arriving for breaking at Kaohsiung on 17 February 1973. The corporate origins of British India can be traced back to The Calcutta & Burmah Steam Navigation Company, created in Glasgow in 1856 to trade along the Indian coast. Expansion in services to the Persian Gulf and south-east Asia led the company's owner, William Mackinnon, to float the British India S. N. Co. Ltd. which was registered in Scotland on 28 October 1862. James Lyle Mackay, latterly the first Earl of Inchcape, responsible for the merger of the P&O and British India S. N. companies in 1914, had ensured the continued corporate identity of British India S. N. until the P&O Group was reorganised in the early 1970s.

(George Wilson)

The ***Sandpiper*** of the General Steam Navigation Co. Ltd. (GSNC) was built at Leith in 1957. She is seen berthed in the East India dock, London. Of just 1324 gross tons, she had operated on GSNC's short sea services until proceeding from Leith on 3 July 1966 bound for Le Havre where she was laid up until purchased by the French Government in March 1967 for a service between the self-governing French territory of St. Pierre & Miquelon and North Sydney, Nova Scotia. Given the new name of ***Ile de Saint Pierre***, she sailed from Le Havre on 8 April 1967 bound for her new home and there giving 13 years' service before being sold to Greece, arriving at Piraeus on 11 November 1980 as ***Alinda***. Following a long period of lay up, she sailed from Piraeus on 1 September 1982 as ***Katia K***. bound for Bahrain and then traded locally in the Persian Gulf. Laid up in a Saudi Arabian port from March 1983, she was reactivated six years later as ***Voyager II*** for a single voyage to Pakistani breakers, arriving at Gadani Beach on 18 April 1989. GSNC was founded in London during the 1820s to link ports in Britain and provide services to north-west continental ports and Iberia. It also operated pleasure cruises down the Thames. GSNC retained its identity after P&O bought a controlling stake in 1920 and played an important role during the 1940 Dunkirk evacuation. As its business declined in the 1960s, GSNC became wholly owned by P&O in 1972 and ceased to be an independent company.

(Ken Wightman, Malcolm Cranfield collection)

Ben Line's **Benalbanach** in Alfred Basin, Birkenhead, in October 1977 during the short lived Ben-Ocean joint service which saw Ben Line ships loading in Birkenhead. **Benalbanach** was the former **Woodarra** of British India S. N., built at Glasgow in 1957 and transferred to P&O in August 1968 to become **Pando Gulf** before being purchased by Ben Line in 1974. William Thomson & Company, founded at Leith in 1847, commenced trading to the Far East in 1859 and became Ben Line Steamers Ltd in 1927. By 1973 the company's first three container ships were delivered for operation within the Trio Group which included OCL, Hapag-Lloyd, Mitsui-OSK and Nippon Yusen Kaisha. By 1978 the Far East trade was fully containerised and the final general cargo ships were sold. **Benalbanach** consequently arrived at Inchon on 21 May 1978 for breaking. Sistership **Benwyvis**, the former **Waroonga**, became **Pando Point** in 1968 before being purchased by Ben Line in 1974 and arriving at Kaohsiung for breaking on 30 January 1978.

(Simon Olsen collection)

12

The **City of Durban** was built in 1954 for Ellerman Lines Ltd by Vickers Armstrong on Tyneside. She was photographed as she hurried down the Esplanade Channel, Durban, in November 1964 during a voyage from Antwerp to Beira. In mid-1971 the four ships of her class, of which *City of Durban* was the last to be delivered, were sold en bloc to M. A. Karageorgis for intended conversion into ferries for service between Patras and Ancona. Although two of the ships were converted as intended the *City of Durban*, renamed *Mediterranean Dolphin*, was instead sent to Kaohsiung in March 1974 for breaking. The origins of Ellerman Lines date from 1892 with the purchase by John Reeves Ellerman of the Liverpool-based Frederick Leyland and Co. Ltd. followed in 1902 by the creation of Ellerman Lines Limited (the former London, Liverpool & Ocean Shipping Co. Ltd.) to own the recently-purchased City Line and Hall Line, both serving the U.K. to India trade. George Smith & Sons of Glasgow had in 1840 started a shipping line which became the City Line Limited in 1890 while Hall Line was founded at Liverpool in 1868 as Sun Shipping by Robert Alexander. In addition, J. R. Ellerman had in 1908 purchased a controlling interest in Henry Bucknall & Son's services between the east coast of the United States, Canada, Australasia and Calcutta, operating from 1914 as Ellerman & Bucknall Steamship. Ellerman Lines expanded into the South and East African trades as well as holding its own in the competitive Indian trade until succumbing to containerisation. In 1966 Ellerman Lines was a founding member of the container line ACT and in 1973 it merged its remaining shipping operations into one division, Ellerman City Liners which in 1987 became Cunard-Ellerman.

(D. K. Shackleton, courtesy Trevor Jones)

The **Derwent** was built by Cammell Laird, Birkenhead, in 1949. The former **Persic** of Shaw, Savill & Albion, she had been renamed in mid-1969 on transfer to Royal Mail Lines and is seen in London's Royal Docks during April 1971 following a round voyage to Auckland for Shaw, Savill & Albion. Before sailing to Bilbao for breaking, where she arrived on 25 November 1971, she had undertaken a final round voyage to Buenos Aires for Royal Mail. In May 1979 Shaw, Savill & Albion took delivery of a new **Derwent**, an improved SD14 type built at Sunderland by Austin & Pickersgill. Employed on Royal Mail Line services to South America, her official ownership was in 1981 changed by the Furness, Withy Group to that of Dee Nav Limited, a company created at Newcastle in 1976 nominally to own three new South Korean-built ships named **Roebuck**, **Ravenswood** and **Riverina**, all of which were sold in 1981. **Derwent** was however sold in mid-1982 to Japanese interests to trade as **Mountain Azalea** until 1988, thereafter changing owners three more times before being broken up at the end of 2002 as the Greek-owned **Alba Sierra**.

(Malcolm Cranfield collection)

Richmond Castle, one of a series built by Harland & Wolff at Belfast for the Union-Castle Mail Steamship Company and delivered in September 1944, is seen on a lay-by berth at Cardiff on 30 May 1971 loaded with a refrigerated cargo from South Africa. She was soon sold for breaking, arriving at Shanghai on 27 August 1971. Union-Castle Mail Steamship Company, formed in 1900 by the merger of Union S.S. Company and the Castle Mail Packet Company, was acquired by the Royal Mail group in 1912. However, following the latter's collapse in 1931, Union-Castle was left with heavy financial commitments, taking several years to recover. In 1956 a new company, British & Commonwealth Shipping Co. Ltd, was formed by the merger of Union-Castle, Bullard King and Clan Line. In 1969 British & Commonwealth invested in Overseas Containers Limited and Union-Castle's remaining conventional cargo ships were sold in 1971. Passenger services ceased in 1977 and reefer services in 1982.

(Malcolm Cranfield)

Port Line's 17-knot **Port St. Lawrence**, built in Belfast in 1961, is seen at speed in United Kingdom waters during June 1963. The photographer was the radio officer on board the passing tanker **Clyde Surveyor**. In June 1975 **Port St. Lawrence** loaded a cargo at London for Calcutta on Brocklebank service; her next voyage on that route was as **Matangi**, albeit in Cunard S. S. ownership. By May 1976 she was moved to services from New Zealand followed, from the end of 1977, by worldwide tramping. While lying off Fujairah in August 1982 she was sold to Greek owners and renamed **Nordave** but was soon sent to Gadani Beach for breaking, arriving there on 30 April 1983. William Milburn had introduced the Port naming system in 1883 with the creation of the Anglo-Australian Steam Navigation Company which in January 1914 amalgamated with J. P. Corry's Star Line, Thos. B. Royden's Indra Line and Tyser Line as the Commonwealth & Dominion Line. The Port Line name evolved after 1916 when, in order to diversify, Cunard bought Commonwealth & Dominion, renaming it Cunard Line Australasian Services and from 1937 Port Line. In 1966 Cunard, in the name of Port Line, joined Ben Line, Blue Star Line, Ellerman Lines and Harrison Line in forming Associated Container Transport (ACT). In 1972 the management of Port Line's vessels was transferred to Cunard-Brocklebank, the last two Port Line ships being transferred to the Brocklebank fleet in 1982.

(Geoffrey Wilson)

Blue Star Line's *Scottish Star* at sea in October 1965. She was built at the Fairfield shipyard in Glasgow in 1950. The photographer had joined the tanker *British Lantern* at Newcastle on 28 July 1965 as radio officer, calling at Aden for bunkers in early October, while *Scottish Star* had sailed from Middlesbrough on 25 September for Bluff, New Zealand, placing her near Aden in early October. In June 1967, at the start of the "Six Day War", *Scottish Star* was one of fourteen ships stranded in the Great Bitter Lake in the Suez Canal and remained there until mid-1975. The ships' crews forged a strong community, exchanging supplies and skills and coordinating their social and sports activities through the Great Bitter Lake Association (GBLA). Two of the ships, *Scottish Star* and *Port Invercargill*, were towed to Piraeus in September 1975 and purchased by Gourdomichalos who had incidentally also purchased *British Lantern* in 1974, renamed *Kavo Vrettanos*. Whereas *Port Invercargill* resumed trading in April 1976 as *Kavo Kolones*, the *Kavo Yerakas* (ex *Scottish Star*) remained at Piraeus until towed to Spain in June 1979 for breaking; coincidentally *Kavo Vrettanos*, laid up at Itea from 8 May 1975, was sent to Spain in January 1979. Blue Star Line, formed in 1911 to carry frozen meat from South America in their own ships, was the creation of the Vestey family who had meat processing interests in South America. The company, which had started to trade to Australia and New Zealand in 1933, was sold in 1998 to P&O Nedlloyd.

(Geoffrey Wilson)

Built by Cammell Laird in 1952, Lamport & Holt Line's **Romney** arrives at Cardiff from Rosario on 25 September 1969. She subsequently arrived at Liverpool on 1 October, spending several weeks in port. Given the frequency of vessel transfers and renamings within the Vestey Group companies, **Romney** was unusual to have had only the one name as which she arrived at Faslane for breaking on 3 October 1978. The name Lamport & Holt derived from an 1845 partnership involving George Holt; his brother Alfred spent a short period with Lamport & Holt before founding Alfred Holt & Company. Trading primarily to the River Plate, Lamport & Holt was acquired in 1911 by Lord Kylsant's competing Royal Mail Group but, following the Kylsant crash, again traded independently until purchased in 1944 by the Vestey Group to operate alongside Blue Star Line and, from 1946, Booth Line. The final ship operating in Lamport & Holt colours was the container ship **Churchill** between 1986 and 1991.

(John Wiltshire)

Bank Line's *Laganbank* is seen outbound from Rotterdam in July 1971. She was built at Belfast in 1955. Initially placed in the nominal ownership of Inver Transport & Trading Co. Ltd., a company created in 1937 as an investment for the Weir and Morton family members separate from their Bank Line shares, she was transferred to Bank Line Ltd in 1964. Sold to Greek owner Theodoros Michael early in 1973 and renamed *Pola Anna*, she was resold in December 1973 to become the Somali-flagged *Golden Sea*. Late in 1974 her owners, Polinnia & Co. Ltd., of Hong Kong, renamed her *Eastern Saturn* as which she sadly foundered on 10 February 1978 during a voyage from Bangkok to Apapa with a cargo of rice. Andrew Weir (who became Lord Inverforth) had started business in 1885 with a sailing ship named *Willowbank*. Bank Line Limited was formed in 1905 to market a growing network of worldwide cargo liner services. For several decades a policy of planned fleet replacement contracted with British shipbuilding yards was pursued. Bank Line's last such order, for six vessels of the "Fish" class, was completed in 1979 but the ships soon became outdated and were sold in the 1980s.

(Simon Olsen collection)

Brocklebank's **Mahout** was built by Alexander Stephen & Sons, Glasgow. We see her departing from London's Royal Docks in February 1971 bound for Dunedin in New Zealand on Port Line service. By 1967 the black hull with white band, with which she and sister ship **Markhor** had been delivered, was painted white with a blue band. The ships were transferred into Cunard ownership in 1968 and the blue band subsequently painted over. Laid up in the River Fal from August 1977, **Mahout** was sold to Greece in 1978 to trade as **Aglaos** until 1980, then as **Evagelia S**. until September 1982 when she was extensively damaged during Iraq/Iran hostilities, stranding 25 miles off Bandar Khomeini. She was subsequently refloated and towed to Bushire but presumably then broken up; **Markhor** was laid up in the River Fal in January 1979 but resumed trading in mid-1980 and was sold a year later to become **Kara Unicorn** until broken up at Dalian in 1984. Essentially founded in Massachusetts in 1770 by Daniel Brocklebank of Whitehaven, the firm of Thos. & Jno. Brocklebank moved to Liverpool in 1819. The Indian service ended in 1977 and Brocklebank ceased trading in 1983.

(Simon Olsen collection)

Dating from 1946, Elders & Fyffes Ltd.'s **Matina** was another product of the Stephen shipyard. She is seen idle at Southampton in September 1968 prior to sailing for the breakers' yard at Ghent, Belgium. She had arrived from Oracabessa in St Mary, Jamaica, east of Ocho Rios, on 12 August. Elders & Fyffes was established in 1901 as a subsidiary of Elder Dempster Shipping of Liverpool with the London fruit distributors Fyffe, Hudson & Co. supplying working capital. In the 1920s, the United Fruit Company of New York had acquired a controlling interest in the company. By acquiring Fyffes' capital and a half share in their main U.S. competitor, the Atlantic Fruit Company of New Orleans, the United Fruit Company had established a virtual monopoly in the trade. Fyffes Group was established in 1969 and United Fruit was merged in 1970 with Eli M. Black's AMK to become the United Brands Company. In 1984, Carl Lindner, Jr. transformed United Brands into Chiquita Brands International.

(Simon Olsen collection)

A. P. Møller's "Hansa B" type **Herta Maersk** was built in Copenhagen. She is seen at Sungai Rejang in Sarawak, Malaysia, on 16 August 1963, photographed from Blue Funnel Line's **Memnon** which the photographer had joined at Hong Kong on 31 July and had sailed from Manila four days earlier. **Herta Maersk** was at that time trading between the Far East and Persian Gulf. As **Spitalertor** she was one of sixteen such ships ordered by the German Government organisation Schiffau Treuhand GmbH on behalf of Hamburg-Amerika Linie and was still building in May 1945 when all unfinished ships were confiscated by Denmark. She was launched on 16 January 1946 but not completed until May 1948. Two later vessels ordered by Schiffau Treuhand but not allocated to German companies were delivered to A. P. Møller as **Emilie Maersk** and **Vibeke Maersk** in February 1947 and April 1948 respectively. In April 1967 all three vessels were transferred to the Liberian flag for operation by A. P. Møller's New York-based Brigantine Transport Corporation, **Herta Maersk** being renamed **Clementine**. "Sold East" early in 1968, she operated until 1977 as **Ping Chau** for Hong Kong Islands Shipping Company, then as **Ocean Speway** for Asean Line, finally being based in Taiwan from 1978 until 1982 as **Lih Fong**. A. P. Møller of Svendborg, for many decades well known as Maersk Line and now the world's largest container line, started business in April 1904 as A/S D/S Svendborg, the nominal owning company of **Herta Maersk**.

(George Wilson)

The **München** of Hamburg-Amerika Linie (HAPAG) was built at Bremen in 1958. We see her inbound for Rotterdam at the end of July 1970. Built for services to the Far East with an overall length of 546ft, gross tonnage of 12,500 and speed of 18 knots, she and her sister ship **Dresden** were larger and faster than the average for that era. In December 1970 both ships were sold to Rickmers Linie, respectively becoming **Etha** and **Sophie Rickmers**, and were broken up in China in 1986.

Hamburg-Amerikanische Packetfahrt-Aktien-Gesellschaft (HAPAG) was established in Hamburg, in 1847. On 1 September 1970, after 123 years of independent existence, HAPAG merged with the Bremen based Norddeutscher Lloyd (North German Lloyd) to form Hapag-Lloyd AG, now one of the world's largest container lines.

(Simon Olsen collection)

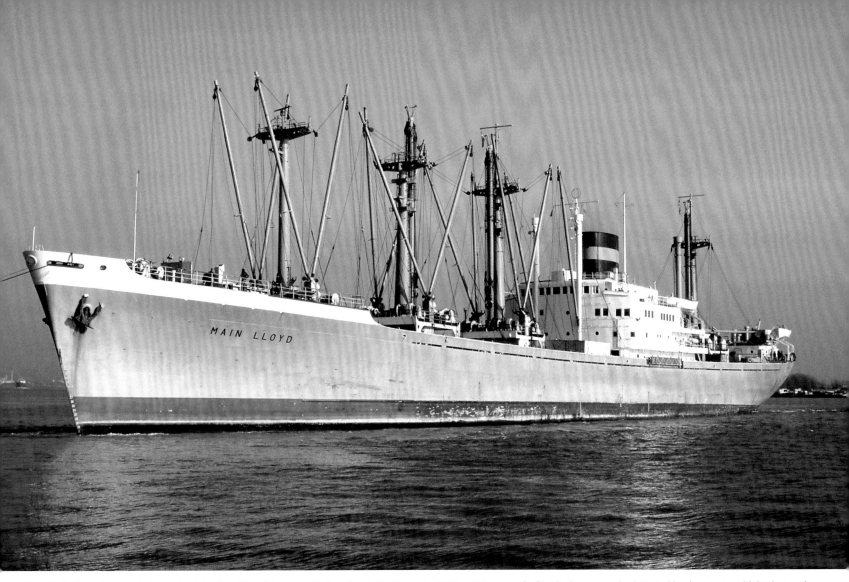

The **Main Lloyd** was photographed in the River Thames off the Royal Docks, London, on arrival in January 1976 during a voyage from Sydney to Hamburg. Built at Rotterdam in 1962 for N.V. Koninklijke Rotterdamsche Lloyd (Royal Rotterdam Lloyd), she became a unit of the Nedlloyd fleet in 1970 and in 1977 was renamed **Nedlloyd Main**. Sold in 1982 to Pacific International Lines Pte. Ltd. of Singapore, she sailed on as **Kota Pusaka** until broken up in China in 1985. Willem Ruys, born in 1809 and the son of a Dutch clergyman, had started business as a shipbroker and shipping agent in 1828 and in 1839 became part owner of a barque, subsequently becoming a major shipowner. The firm of Wm. Ruys & Sons was created in 1870 and Royal Rotterdam Lloyd in 1883. The company's independence came to an end in 1970 when absorbed into Nedlloyd, later into P&O Nedlloyd and then Maersk.

(Dave Salisbury)

Wilh, Wilhelmsen's *Talleyrand*, passing Rozenburg inbound for Rotterdam, in June 1971, was built at Gothenburg in 1949. Mainly trading between the USA or Europe and the Far East, at the end of 1971 she was sold to the Uruguay-based Greek owner Angelos Politis to trade as *Minerva* until arriving at Gadani Beach, Pakistan, for breaking on 15 September 1978. The Wilhelmsen family from Tønsberg, Norway, had started business in 1861 and extended into cargo liner services from 1901, moving to Oslo in 1918. In 1969, together with Fearnley & Eger and A. F. Klaveness, Wilh. Wilhelmsen established Barber Lines to market their United States-based liner services and in 1974 Barber Lines joined with Blue Sea Line (Blue Funnel and Seaco – Swedish East Asia) to create Barber Blue Sea Line, a joint venture which came to an end in 1989.

(Simon Olsen collection)

The **Yang-Tse** of Messageries Maritimes was built at La Ciotat in 1958. We see her sailing from Le Havre on 31 August 1969 during a voyage from Antwerp, Le Havre, La Pallice and Marseille to Lourenço Marques (now Maputo) in Mozambique. After arriving at Hong Kong on 10 March 1978 she was reported as sold for further trading as **Lidia H.** but instead sailed on 24 May 1978 bound for Tsingtao (now Qingdao) for intended breaking. However, she was there acquired by China Ocean Shipping Company to trade locally as **Lu Hai 65**, from 1982 operated by Shandong Province Marine Shipping Company. While her ultimate fate is unknown she was presumably broken up before 1986 when a new ship of the same name was acquired. In 1835 the French Government had created a steamship service between Marseilles and the Levant. After the Franco-Prussian War and the abolition of the monarchy in 1871, the company became Compagnie des Messageries Maritimes. The fleet was rebuilt following the Second World War but between 1969 and 1972 passenger services were closed and in 1977 Messageries Maritimes, together with Compagnie Générale Transatlantique, became part of Compagnie Générale Maritime and from 1998 part of CMA CGM, one of the world's top container lines.

(Simon Olsen collection)

We now look at freighters in a variety of ports. Ellerman Lines' *Arcadian*, the last ship with a Papayanni name, was built at Leith in 1960. She was discharging cargo from the eastern Mediterranean at Newhaven, East Sussex, in September 1972. The trade name of Ellerman & Papayanni continued to be used by Ellerman Lines until the *Catanian* and *Florian* were laid up at Liverpool in August 1971 and soon sold. *Arcadian* was renamed *City of Famagusta* in 1974 and sold in 1977 to Associated Levant Lines of Beirut. As *Batroun* she traded uneventfully until sold for breaking at Gadani Beach where she arrived on 18 December 1986. Ellerman & Papayanni Line was formed in 1901 when Papayanni Steamship Company joined the newly-created London, Liverpool and Ocean Shipping Company, which in 1902 changed its name to Ellerman Lines.

(Malcolm Cranfield collection)

Blue Star Line's **California Star** was built at Belfast in 1945. We see her in London's Royal Docks on 4 March 1967. She subsequently sailed on 11 March 1967 bound for Auckland and Lyttelton. She was laid up in the River Blackwater, Essex, on 14 July 1967 but was returned to service on 27 October 1967, possibly due to a need for additional tonnage following the closure of the Suez Canal. A reported sale to Far East buyers, for conversion to a fish factory ship, having failed, on 22 June 1968 she sailed from London for Sydney via Cape Town, reportedly sold to Taiwan breakers.

However, she returned to London, arriving there on 16 November and eventually arriving at Kaohsiung for breaking on 21 April 1969. Built as **Empire Clarendon**, she was purchased by the Vestey Group's Frederick Leyland & Co Ltd in 1947 to trade as **Tuscan Star**, then from 1948 as **Timaru Star**. Her nominal ownership was changed in 1950 to Lamport & Holt and she was renamed **California Star** in 1958 on transfer to Blue Star Limited.

(Simon Olsen collection)

Bibby Line's **Shropshire** was built at the Fairfield shipyard in Govan in 1959. She is seen berthed in mid Huskisson 3 Branch Dock, Liverpool, on 19 March 1972, from the remarkable vantage point of the top of the jib of a roof-mounted crane on the opposite side of the dock. She had arrived at Liverpool from Tamatave, Madagascar, on 24 February, presumably with a cargo of sugar for the Tate & Lyle refinery. The ships berthed in West Canada dock (long since used for scrap metal) were **Benarkle** and **Indian Splendour** while the smoky ship on the adjacent berth was the 1957-built **Elias Lemos**. **Shropshire**, which had often been employed on charter to other lines, such as Ellerman and CSAV of Chile, was sold later in 1972 to Halcoussis who traded her as **Argiro** until laid up at Piraeus in October 1981. She was reactivated at the end of 1984 for a final voyage to Chittagong for breaking as **Naftilos**. Sistership **Yorkshire**, sold in January 1971 to Ramon de La Sota Jr. to trade for ten years as **Bordabekoa**, was broken up at Alang in May 1984 as **Sea Reliance**. Bibby, shipowners since 1807, had started a service to Egypt, Colombo and Rangoon in 1891 which ceased in 1971.

(Paul Boot)

The ***Morshansk*** of the U.S.S.R.'s Black Sea Shipping Company is an example of the B44 type and was built at Gdansk in 1964. She is seen moving through the Hornby Cut in Liverpool docks in October 1975, probably to berth in South Alexandra 2 Branch Dock to discharge a cargo of animal feedstuffs. She had earlier passed through the Suez Canal on 12 October bound for the River Mersey. In December 1988 ***Morshansk*** was sold at Hong Kong to trade briefly under the St. Vincent and Grenadines flag as ***Merula*** until beached for breaking at Alang, India, on 19 May 1989. The Black Sea Shipping Company of Odessa, founded in 1833, had retained its identity during the Communist era from 1917 to 1991, emerging as the privately owned BLASCO and trading worldwide until its collapse in 1995.

(David Worthy, Malcolm Cranfield collection)

The **Irish Poplar** of Dublin-based Irish Shipping Limited is seen berthed in Alexandra 3 Branch Dock, Liverpool, on 27 June 1972. She had sailed from Buenos Aires on 22 May bound for Liverpool via Santos. A 16 knot steam turbine ship built at Birkenhead in 1956 by Cammell, Laird & Co., she was the only ship in the Irish Shipping fleet registered at Waterford. **Irish Poplar** was sold in December 1972 to the Greek owner Theodoros Michael, later the buyer of **Laganbank** (page 18) and **Raphael** (page 33), who traded her as **Polamary** until reselling the ship one year later to Taiwan's Char Hwa Marine Co. As **Golden Lion** she was broken up at Kaohsiung, arriving there on 15 June 1979, coincidentally just two months after an earlier **Golden Lion**, the former **Wharanui**, Guan Guan owned and built in 1956 at Clydebank. Sistership **Irish Spruce**, which was registered at Cork, had been wrecked on 26 January 1972 off Quita Sueño Bank, a reef formation near Nicaragua, during a voyage from Callao to New Orleans with a cargo of lead, zinc and copper concentrates and coffee.

(Paul Boot)

The **Eva Jeanette**, built in 1958 in Stockholm for Swedish owner A/B Bonnierföretagen which had recently been purchased by A/B Transmarin, is seen at Liverpool in the summer of 1965 while on time charter to Cunard Line for its services to Canada. Erik Kekonius of Halmstad, who in 1945 had started a factory for paper products named Billingsfors Långed A/B, had entered shipowning in 1954 as Lion S. S. Co. A/B with two small ships named **Jeanette** and **Charlotte**, both managed by Arnold de Champs of Stockholm. In 1955 he invested in a larger ship, named **Jacqueline**, the former **Jersey City** of Reardon Smith, which was sold to Poland in 1959. Meanwhile, in 1957, shortly before the new **Eva Jeanette** was delivered, he sold the two small ships and renamed Lion S. S. as A/B Bonnierföretagen, basing it at Stockholm, and he also took control of the old established Adolf Bratt & Co. Replacements for **Charlotte** and **Jacqueline** were purchased in 1959/60 but sold four years later, and in 1965 he relinquished control of Bratt to TOR Line, as he focused on managing his passenger and car ferry operation Lion Ferry A/B, which was however taken over by Stena in 1983. Soon after the Cunard charter had ended in 1966, **Eva Jeanette** was given the Transmarin name **Wanja** and in 1973 **Martina**. Sold to Greece in 1978 with a long term charter to Deutsche Nah-Ost, she was renamed **Skopelos Star** in 1981 and beached for breaking at Chittagong on 21 January 1984.

(Malcolm Cranfield collection)

The *Ragni Paulin*, owned by Paulins Rederi Ab of Turku, Finland, and built in Dundee in 1943, was discharging a cargo of grain at Birkenhead's East Float in July 1966. This was her third consecutive voyage with grain from Canada to U.K. ports. She subsequently sailed from Birkenhead on 10 August bound for Igarka in Russia to load a cargo of timber. *Ragni Paulin* had been built under private contract as *Norman Monarch* for Raeburn & Verel's Monarch Line of Glasgow and purchased by Paulin in 1957. She was sold to Chinese breakers in September 1969 but may have continued trading locally. A sister ship, *Scottish Monarch*, was sold in the same year to a Greek buyer who renamed her *Demetrius D.S.* but resold her to China in 1958 and, under her final name of *Zhan Dou 55*, is believed to have survived well into the 1970s; the only known fact is that she was broken up prior to 1985. Johan Werner Paulin had commenced shipowning in 1916 with the purchase of the 1872-built *Alexa*, which survived until 1933, and concluded with the 1967-built bulk carrier *Stormqueen*, sold in 1971.

(Norman Hesketh)

It was unusual for Lamport & Holt to charter ships to other lines. However the *Raphael*, built at the Bartram shipyard in Sunderland in 1953, is here seen at Birkenhead on 7 April 1973 loading cargo for East Africa in Harrison Line colours. The odd nature of the arrangement was compounded by the fact that the Pakistan-owned *Mansoor* was chartered by Lamport & Holt to simultaneously load a cargo at Birkenhead for Santos. *Raphael* was sold at Liverpool in June 1976 to the Greek buyer Theodoros Michael who had in 1973 purchased *Laganbank* (page 18) and *Cedarbank* from

Andrew Weir, the latter being renamed *Pola Monika*. Neither ship survived for long. *Raphael*, renamed *Pola Rika*, spent over twelve months at Lagos from February 1978 before sailing to Gijón in Spain for breaking, arriving there on 30 May 1979, *Pola Monika* meanwhile being broken up in Pakistan. Having already quickly sold *Pola Anna*, the former *Laganbank*, and *Polamary*, the former *Irish Poplar* (page 30), a fifth and final ship, *Pola Nina*, the former *Loa* purchased from CSAV of Chile in mid-1977, was sold at the end of 1978.

(Paul Boot)

The occasional use by Lamport & Holt of ships owned by other lines within the Vestey Group is exemplified by Booth Line's *Rubens*, built in Sunderland at the Wm. Pickersgill shipyard in 1951. Unusually seen in Garston Dock on 2 July 1972, she had sailed from Buenos Aires on 15 May bound for Liverpool via Itajai and by 20 August was back on the Brazilian coast loading her next cargo. *Rubens* was by then among the last of the steam reciprocating powered cargo liners still in service. The photographer was given a tour of her antiquated engine room in July 1973.

Delivered to Booth Line in August 1951 as *Crispin*, she was transferred in 1953 to Austasia Line and renamed *Mandowi* to operate between Australia and Far East ports. Reverting to Booth ownership in June 1966, she sailed as *Dunstan* between the United States and Brazil until January 1967 when renamed *Rubens* under Lamport & Holt management. Towards the end of 1973 she was sold to George Kalogeras of Piraeus who very briefly traded her as *Irini K*. Beached at Istanbul on 24 April 1974, her remains were still visible in December 1975.

(Paul Boot)

The ***Salaverry*** of the Pacific Steam Navigation Company (PSNC) was built by Harland & Wolff at Belfast in 1946. She is seen in Avonmouth's Old Dock on 19 February 1971 as ***Pelias***, the name she was given at Manchester in July 1967 on purchase by Stravelakis Brothers, of Piraeus and London. She was discharging a cargo of grain from the Black Sea and sailed two days later. Between 1940 and 1944 Harland & Wolff had built a series of similar ships for Royal Mail Lines starting with ***Pardo***. In 1943 PSNC obtained a licence to build two identical ships, ***Samanco*** and ***Sarmiento***, and these were followed post-war by four similar ships including ***Salaverry***, concluding with ***Salamanca*** in 1948. While PSNC's service from the U.K. to the west coast of South America had commenced in 1840, the company was linked with Royal Mail Lines from 1910 until 1984 when both names disappeared within the Furness Withy Group which had taken them over in 1965. PSNC's services were operated during much of the 1970s by the 1966-built ***Orcoma*** and the three 1973 sister ships ***Orbita***, ***Orduna*** and ***Ortega***, also built by Cammell Laird. New ships named ***Oropesa*** and ***Oroya*** were delivered by the Lithgow shipyard in 1978 while in 1980 ***Ortega*** was renamed ***Andes***, a name repeated when a new containership was delivered in 1984. ***Pelias*** sadly foundered in heavy weather on 12 December 1972 in a position 250 miles south-east of Durban during a voyage from Maceió (Brazil) to Saigon with a cargo of sugar.

(Malcolm Cranfield)

Federal Steam Navigation Company's *Rakaia* was another product of the Harland & Wolff shipyard. She is unusually seen in Avonmouth's oil basin, laying by on 4 December 1970 prior to sailing on the next tide for London to load for New Zealand ports. *Rakaia* returned to London on 14 April 1971 and arrived at Hong Kong for breaking on 22 August 1971. One of four refrigerated cargo liners built at Belfast in 1945/6 and originally named *Empire Abercorn*, she was purchased in 1946 by New Zealand Shipping Company (NZSC) and transferred to Federal S. N. in 1966. The other three ships later became *Port Hobart*, *Empire Star* and sister ship *California*

Star (page 27). Federal S. N., formed by Birt, Potter & Hughes in 1895, had Australian conference trading rights and although taken over by NZSC in 1912, continued to trade as a separate concern, albeit with common NZSC management, even after the latter's acquisition by P&O in 1916. In 1966, in advance of containerisation, a rationalisation process started with a tax efficient merging of corporate ownership culminating in full absorption into P&O in 1973 when the operation of their last ships was transferred to P&O's newly-formed General Cargo Division.

(Malcolm Cranfield)

Clan Line's **Clan Maclay** was built at Greenock in 1949. In this atmospheric view of Avonmouth in its busy heyday, she was berthed second off from Elder Dempster Lines' **Ebani** at West Wharf on 13 March 1973. **Ebani** had arrived on 7 March from Lagos, **Clan Maclay** on 10 March from Madras. **Clan Maclay** was sold at Liverpool early in 1976 to the Maldives Government to trade as **Climax Amethyst** until renamed **Angelos** early in 1979, shortly before being sent to Kaohsiung for breaking in May 1979. The origins of Clan Line go back to 1877 when C. W. Cayzer & Company commenced business in Liverpool, trading from the U.K. to India. The company became Cayzer, Irvine & Company in 1878 and moved to Glasgow in 1881 when the Clan Line Association of Steamers was formed. Clan Line's last ships were sold in 1981.

(John Wiltshire)

Moss Hutchison Line's *Amarna* was built at Belfast in 1949. She is seen discharging cargo at R Shed, Avonmouth, in the late 1960s with a Bristol City Line ship astern. *Amarna* had normally operated to the eastern Mediterranean but was chartered out to Cunard between April and December 1967 for services to Canada as *Assyria*. In 1973 the Moss Hutchison fleet was transferred to P&O and by 1976 only the newest two ships, *Melita* and *Makaria*, remained in the fleet, oddly retaining Moss Hutchison colours until sold in 1979. *Amarna* was sold in 1975 to Grecomar Shipping Agency for employment mainly for the carriage of cement from Black Sea ports to Egypt. Renamed *Kastriani III*, her final sailing from Constantza was late in 1982. Sold to clients of Anglo Trading of Bristol, she arrived at Aden on 6 November to be renamed *Montrose* but instead was eventually sent to Gadani Beach for breaking, sailing from Aden on 16 January 1984.

(R. M. Parsons, courtesy of John D. Hill)

The **Pinemore** of Johnston Warren Lines was built at Burntisland in 1955. Operated by Prince Line from 1964 as **African Prince**, she is seen alongside a repair jetty at Newport, South Wales, on 27 March 1971 while in course of sale to the Maldives Government. She had been laid up at Falmouth from 13 January 1971 pending sale. The Prince of Wales's feathers, welded on her funnel and painted white, have already been removed and she departed from Newport on 27 April 1971 bound for Rotterdam to load her first cargo as **Maldive Mail**, retaining her British registry. On 31 May 1975, during a voyage from Karachi to Singapore, she suffered a fire off Veraval, India, and was subsequently wrecked. James Knott of Newcastle, who started business in 1878 and had named his first steamer **Saxon Prince**, had in 1884 created Prince Steam Shipping and in 1895 Prince Line Limited. In 1916, after losing his three sons in the First World War, he sold the company to Furness, Withy & Co., the subsequent owner of Johnston Warren Lines.

(Malcolm Cranfield)

Ropner Shipping Co.'s **Bellerby** was a standard prefabricated B- type, built in 1944 by Wm. Gray at West Hartlepool as **Empire Irving** and purchased from the British Government in 1946. She is seen laid up in No.1 Dock, Barry, towards the end of the 1950s. She was sold to Iran in 1960 to trade as **Persian Cambyses** until 1964, then briefly as **Iranian Trader** before being renamed **Shiraz**. Having arrived at Dammam on 7 May 1966 with about 3000 tonnes of wheat loaded at New Orleans, **Shiraz** was placed under arrest and lay derelict until January 1970 when beached after breaking her moorings. Following her sale in September 1970 arrangements were made to tow the ship, renamed **Sayhet**, to Bahrain in order to dump her cargo and be fumigated. **Sayhet** was eventually towed to Gadani Beach in December 1972 for breaking. Sir Robert Ropner, having emigrated from Magdeburg and worked in partnership with Thomas Appleby, had set up his own business in West Hartlepool in 1874. Before both world wars a large fleet of tramp ships had been established and in 1946 the company launched a cargo liner service from the UK to US Gulf ports. Investments in tankers commenced in the mid-1950s and in bulk carriers from the mid-1960s. The Ropner company was taken over by Jacobs Holdings Plc in 1997.

(Malcolm Cranfield collection)

Edwin Reith is seen berthed at the top of the eastern end of King's Dock, Swansea, on 15 June 1968, loading cargo for Canada and the United States during a time charter to Bristol City Line which lasted until January 1971. Built at Rendsburg in 1958 for „Orion" Schiffahrts-Gesellschaft Reith & Co., *Edwin Reith* and sister ship *Magdalena Reith* were sold together in 1972/3 to Sun-Line Ltd of Hong Kong and, following resale in 1979 to Chan Ching Pan's Joint Maritime Co., arrived at Shanghai together at the end of 1984 for breaking. „Orion" Schiffahrts GmbH was created in 1931 at Rostock as a partnership of ship owners Ernst Behnke and Erik Larsen. In October 1939, due to problems with the local Nazis, Ernst Behnke, who from 1934 was Orion's sole owner, relocated the business to Hamburg. After the war ended he invited Hans-Edwin Reith, a former submarine commander and grandson of shipowner Johann M. K. Blumenthal, to join Orion as a partner. In 1949 Rudolf A. Oetker and Alfred Kühne supplied fresh capital and in 1951 the company was renamed „Orion" Schiffahrts-Gesellschaft Reith & Co. From 1954 Reith was sole owner of Orion and in 1959 bought Blumenthal's failing business, then owned by son-in-law Walter John Böge, providing new tonnage from 1968. After a decade of declining fortunes for Orion, Hans-Edwin Reith died in 1987. However, from the early 1990s, his sons Johann-Stephan and Matthias-Kaspar began a substantial newbuilding programme and Johann-Stephan now operates a substantial fleet of ships as Orion Bulkers. Since 2005 Matthias-Kaspar has independently built up a fleet of ships under the name J. M. K. Blumenthal GmbH.

(John Wiltshire)

Houlder Brothers' *Queensbury* is seen loading locally manufactured steel or tinplate products at Swansea on 22 September 1969 during a voyage from Liverpool to Rosario. Nominally owned by Alexander Shipping Company, in which Houlder Brothers had invested in 1937 and had wholly owned from 1947, *Queensbury* was built at Burntisland in 1953. She was followed between 1958 and 1960 by the similar *Shaftesbury*, *Tewkesbury* and *Westbury*. Alexander Shipping Company was formed in 1874 and participated in the coal trade out of the South Wales ports, often for South America. The 1931-built *Queensbury* became a war loss in 1941 during a return voyage from Buenos Aires to London with a cargo of grain and general cargo. In the autumn of 1971 *Queensbury* was laid up at Liverpool alongside the joint Houlder Line and Empire Transport Company's owned *Swan River* pending their sale. Both ships sailed in December 1971, *Queensbury* as the Greek-owned *Sandra* and *Swan River* as the Maldives-owned *Premier Atlantic*. After spending the first half of 1973 under repair at Piraeus, *Sandra* sailed for Shanghai where she was "sold East", taking the name *Fong Lee*. In mid 1976 she became *Lien Chang* as which she arrived at Kaohsiung on 18 November 1978 for breaking.

(John Wiltshire)

The **Høegh Meling** is seen in King George V Dock, Glasgow, towards the end of July 1973 loading cargo for Warri and Sapele, having arrived on 24 July from Newport. The crane in the background is in the Charles Connell shipyard across the river. *Høegh Meling* was built at Landskrona in 1955 and owned by Skibs A/S Corona (H. M. Wrangell) of Haugesund and was on long term charter to Leif Høegh & Co. A/S of Oslo, one of the UK/West Africa conference lines. Having taken the name **Høegh Meling** in September 1969, her original name of **Lars Meling** was restored in April 1977 but she was sold at the end of 1977 to Navegante Shipping Agencies Ltd of Hong Kong. Renamed **Santa Lucia II**, she sailed from Antwerp on 30 December for Warri and then to the Far East where, in mid-1978, she was further renamed **Nelia**. Having arrived at Huangpu, Shanghai, on 29 February 1984, she was reported in July 1984 to have been broken up there.

(Malcolm Cranfield collection)

The U.S.S.R.'s Northern Shipping Company was based in Archangel. Its **Irshales**, built at Turku in 1962, is in Grangemouth lock on 7 July 1975 outbound for Garston to discharge the balance of her cargo of timber from Archangel, having arrived on 30 June to discharge the cargo stowed on deck. She was an early example of a series of similar ships built in Finland for the U.S.S.R. between 1961 and 1971. *Irshales* was sold in 1989 to Albahria Shipping & Trading Company of Alexandria, Egypt, which traded her as **Nasr Allah** until beached for breaking at Bombay on 12 May 1994. Founded in 1870, the Northern Shipping Company is one of the oldest shipping companies in Russia. The lock serving Grangemouth docks, on the River Forth near Falkirk, leads directly into the oil dock but is some distance away from the port's dry cargo operations.

(Malcolm Cranfield collection)

Dating from 1950, Moss Hutchison Line's *Kypros* was another ship built at the Sunderland shipyard of Wm. Pickersgill. She was photographed at Glasgow, in Queen's Dock on the north side of the River Clyde, in March 1969. Just visible behind her stern is the stone embankment on which trains run to Helensburgh. Queens Dock, completed in March 1880, was filled in during November 1977 using rubble from the demolition of St. Enoch Station. The Scottish Exhibition and Conference Centre has since been built on the site. Moss Hutchison Line Limited, registered in 1934, had arisen from an amalgamation of James Moss & Company (Moss Line) and J. & P. Hutchison following the collapse of the Royal Mail Group. However, its ownership passed in 1935 to the General Steam Navigation Company which was wholly owned by P&O. During the second half of 1967 *Kypros* was chartered out to Cunard as *Aurania* for services to Canada. She was sent to Piraeus in August 1976 to join the Grecomar fleet as *Angeliki*. Late in 1981 her name was abbreviated to *Angel* for a voyage to Mokha, Yemen, from where she proceeded to Beypore in India for breaking, being beached there in April 1982.

(Malcolm Cranfield collection)

The **Sloterdyk** of Nederlandsch-Amerikaansche Stoomvaart Mij (NASM) (Holland America Line) was built at Odense in 1939. We see her at Antwerp in August 1964. She had sailed from Hamburg on 13 August 1964 bound for Galveston, passing Lizard on 21 August. Having been launched on 30 September 1969, she was delivered to NASM in March 1940, just a few days before the German invasion of Denmark (Operation Weserübung) on 9 April. She was being operated under the jurisdiction of the British Ministry of War Transport when the United States entered the war in December 1941. Having left New York on 9 January 1942, she eventually returned there in August 1942 and was converted into a troopship by Sullivan Drydock & Repair Corp. She made a final voyage with troops, from San Francisco on 1 December 1945 to Manila, returning on 16 January 1946. She was then released by the Army, sailing to Vancouver to load for the Dutch East Indies. After a final voyage from Hamburg to New York early in 1966, she was sent to Bilbao for breaking, arriving there on 30 March 1966. Sister ship **Sommelsdyk**, which was delivered in September 1939, continued in service during wartime as a freighter before being used to carry troops. After a final voyage from Galveston to Rotterdam in May 1965, her name was shortened to **Somme** for the short voyage to the breakers, arriving at Burriana on 11 June 1965. NASM was formed at Rotterdam in 1873, in 1971 becoming known as Holland-Amerika Lijn but in 1973 disposing of its cargo division to concentrate on passenger ships. It ceased operating as a Dutch line in 1989 when purchased by Carnival.

(Malcolm Cranfield collection)

The **Rheinfels** of Deutsche Dampfschiffahrts-Gesellschaft "Hansa" was built at the Charles Connell shipyard in Glasgow in 1941. She is seen in Überseehafen at her home port of Bremen in December 1958, towed by the tug **Elsfleth** built locally in 1929. **Rheinfels**, built as **Empire Rennie**, was purchased in 1956 from Van Nievelt, Goudriaan of Rotterdam which had operated her as **Alchiba** since 1946 following four years of war service with the Dutch Government as **Frans Hals**. In 1968 she was sold to Sigalas & Platis of Piraeus who traded her as **Peramataris** until broken up near her home port in February 1979. Despite suffering an engine room fire when off Malta on 6 June 1975 during a voyage to Lagos with a cargo of cement, she successfully completed that last loaded voyage in 1976 but was then laid up.

(Karl-Josef Hagenkötter collection)

Shaw, Savill & Albion Line's **Coptic** is berthed at Wellington in October 1964. She was built at Wallsend in 1928. Other than suffering a minor collision with HMAS **Adelaide** in September 1940 the **Coptic**, along with **Taranaki** and **Karamea**, survived the war unscathed while **Zealandic** was torpedoed in 1941. **Coptic** had sailed from Hamburg on 30 May 1964 for Dunedin and Bluff and was loading a return cargo to Glasgow. Following one more round voyage from Liverpool to Brisbane, returning to London, she was sent to breakers at Antwerp, arriving there on 14 July 1965. While the Albion Line had started business at Glasgow in 1856, Robert Shaw and Walter Savill,

employed in London by shipbrokers in the New Zealand trade, had formed Shaw, Savill & Co. in 1858. The combined Shaw, Savill & Albion Line, created in 1882, had from 1884 to 1933 operated a joint service to New Zealand together with the Oceanic Steam Navigation Company's White Star Line, holding company for Kylsant's empire. Following the Kylsant crash in 1931, Furness Withy also took control of Shaw, Savill & Albion as well as taking a substantial holding in Royal Mail Lines, purchased outright in 1965. Shaw Savill & Albion, which continued to use White Star-style names ending ic, ceased to be a shipowning company in 1984.

(Ian Shiffman collection)

The **Degema** of Elder Dempster Lines was built at West Hartlepool in 1959. We see her at Philadelphia on 29 April 1972 loading cargo for Freetown and Duala. She was unusual in having a 10-ton swl Thompson derrick which is understood to have been fitted at Greenock in mid-1966 as an experiment at the instigation of Marine Superintendent Capt. Pari Hughes. It has been said that the derrick was quite slow for working general cargo but had the advantage of not requiring guys or powered topping lifts on other winches if being used for lifts which had to be placed at different parts of the hatch, which was very useful when loading logs. In February 1979 **Degema** was sold at Tilbury to S. C. Vazeos of Piraeus and renamed **Veejumbo**, a name possibly chosen due to her Thompson derrick which resembled a jumbo derrick. Laid up at Piraeus from 9 July 1981, she sailed on 6 November 1982 bound for Karachi as **Degema** and was beached for breaking on 30 January 1983.

(Malcolm Cranfield collection)

The **Manchester City** of Manchester Liners was built in 1937 by the Blythswood Shipbuilding Co. Ltd. at Scotstoun. She is seen berthed alongside Searle's grain elevator at Fort William, Northern Ontario, Canada, on 21 July 1962. Located on the Kaministiquia River at its entrance to Lake Superior, in January 1970 Fort William amalgamated with Port Arthur to form the city of Thunder Bay. Following the opening of the Manchester Ship Canal in 1894, making it possible for large ocean-going ships to sail directly into the heart of Manchester, Sir Christopher Furness, of Furness Withy & Company, had proposed in 1897 that a Manchester-based shipping line should be formed. The public prospectus for Manchester Liners Ltd was issued on 10 May 1898 and Furness Withy became the largest shareholder. Manchester Liners decided from the outset to make Canada their prime route, with a secondary route to the southern United States cotton ports. By the late 1960s rising costs, strikes and restrictive practices on both sides of the Atlantic, plus subsidised competition from American shipping lines, persuaded Manchester Liners to invest in containerships. **Manchester City** arrived at Faslane for breaking on 15 May 1964.

(A. Schelling, René Beauchamp collection)

Peninsular Shipping Company's *Greenford* was built in 1949 by Smith's Dock, Middlesbrough, as *Amakura* for Booker Line of Liverpool. Purchased by Peninsular in 1961, she is seen working cargo from barges at Singapore on 19 August 1963. Her continued Liverpool registration had disguised her beneficial ownership by the People's Republic of China. Peninsular had been created in Hong Kong in 1958 as a vehicle for China purchasing the 1943-built *Fort St. Paul*, renamed *Longford* but immediately transferred to China as *Ho Ping 50*, and the 1930-built *Fairford* which was transferred to China in 1960. Seven ships including *Greenford* were subsequently registered in the Peninsular name between 1960 and 1964 culminating in the newly-built *Peony*. Peninsular, managed from Hong Kong by Ocean Tramping Co. Ltd., was again used for the purchase of four ships by China between 1976 and 1979 and finally one in 1985, the 1970 bulk carrier *Pratincole*, which was renamed *Hope Sea* in 1994. Booker Line was formed in 1911, principally to operate cargo and passenger services between Liverpool and British Guiana in the West Indies.

(George Wilson)

Ocean Steamship Company's *Ixion* and F. C. Strick's *Armanistan* were bunkering at Aden on 11 February 1963. The photographer was on board Blue Funnel Line's *Autolycus* on passage from Birkenhead to Singapore to join *Charon* as surgeon. Throughout 1960 he had served on board the *Ixion*, built in Belfast in 1951, considering her his best posting. While *Ixion* served Ocean continuously until broken up in Spain during 1972, the *Armanistan*, built at South Shields in 1949, was sold in 1965 to the London-based Expedo & Co. and placed under the Liberian flag as *Conway*. Expedo, managed by Thomas Hsu, soon focused on tankers, from 1974 to 1982 also managing the 74000dwt *Burmah Spar* (ex *Saga Sky*) and then participating in the creation of Teekay Shipping. *Conway* was therefore sold in 1967 to Vas. Kaminis of Piraeus to trade as *Mitera Maria*. In April 1971 she was sold to Fouad Khayat of Beirut and renamed *Marbella* but suffered an engine room fire at Karachi in February 1973 and was broken up locally.

(George Wilson)

Brocklebank's steam turbine powered *Masirah*, built in 1957 at the Port Glasgow shipyard of William Hamilton & Company, is seen working cargo at Colombo, Ceylon, on 12 September 1963 and was photographed from Blue Funnel Line's *Memnon*. *Masirah* had sailed from Calcutta on 24 August 1963 for Antwerp; on her next voyage from Calcutta she loaded for Houston. Laid up at Falmouth from June 1971, *Masirah* was sold by the end of that year to Marchessini of Greece which had also purchased two of her four sisterships, the 1959-built *Mangla* and 1960-built *Mathura*, for liner services from Europe and/or the east coast of the United States to the Far East. Renamed *Eurysthenes*, on 25 April 1974 she was sadly wrecked on Calantas Rock in the San Bernardino Strait, Philippines, during a voyage from Hamburg and Charleston to Yokohama. After refloating she was towed to Kaohsiung for breaking. Brocklebank's Indian services ended in 1977.

(George Wilson)

We now look at freighters in rivers, waterways and port approaches. Photographed passing Gravesend on 31 May 1971 with a telephoto lens from Clifton Marine Parade in Rosherville, opposite Tilbury landing stage, is Strick Line's classic *Tangistan* inbound for London's Royal Docks from Antwerp to load for Abu Dhabi. She was built in 1950 at the South Shields shipyard of John Readhead. Best known for its cargo liner services between the United Kingdom and Persian/Arabian Gulf ports, Strick Line was founded in 1887 by Frank C. Strick of Swansea. *Tangistan*, the last of the seven magnificent post-war steamships delivered by Readhead between 1947 and 1950, which also included *Armanistan* (see page 49), was also the last to be sold, for breaking at Kaohsiung where she arrived on 13 March 1972. Although a controlling interest in Strick was acquired by Lord Inchcape, chairman of P&O, the company retained its independence and in 1928 Frank C. Strick resumed a 49% interest. However, in 1972, P&O reacquired the Strick minority interests and proceeded to absorb the Strick fleet and operations into its General Cargo Division, giving the remaining ships names commencing *Strath*.

(Simon Olsen collection)

Tilbury on the River Thames, although south facing, is a good location for ship photography, inward ships passing at fairly close quarters. The **Leiderkerk**, built at Schiedam in 1959 and owned by United Netherlands, is seen passing Tilbury Fort, inbound for London, in September 1971. She was sold to Golden Union Shipping Co. of Greece in 1978 to trade as **Sea Glory** until mid-1979 when renamed **Tom**. In September 1980 she arrived at Umm Qasr near Basrah, Iraq, just as hostilities commenced between Iraq and Iran, trapping her in port. She was released late in 1988 and towed to Alang for breaking. United Netherlands - N.V. Vereenigde Nederlandsche Scheepvaartmaatschappij (VNS) - was founded in April 1920 as a unique collaboration between eight Dutch shipping companies to operate various liner services, independently managed until 1940 but after 1945 managed by VNS. In 1970 VNS merged with several other Dutch shipping companies to form the Nedlloyd Group, which in 1977 became Royal Nedlloyd, in 1996 itself merging with P&O Containers Ltd., then buying out P&O's interest in 2004 before being taken over by Maersk in 2005.

(C. C. Beazley, Malcolm Cranfield collection)

Gallions Reach in North Woolwich, where ships using London's Royal Docks manoeuvred into and out of the King George V entrance lock, was a busy stretch of the River Thames, and so a favourite location for ship photography until the end of the 1970s. Ships departing from the lock entered the river stern first. After the last trading vessel departed on 7 December 1981 the docks were briefly used as a lay up facility. The Royal Albert Dock, accessed through a cut, runs parallel to King George V Dock; Victoria Dock lies beyond that to the west. Clan Line's **Clan Macdougall** built in 1944 at the Cartsdyke shipyard in Greenock, is seen sailing from the Royal Docks in March 1970 bound for Cape Town. Her final voyage from London started on 7 October 1971, under the Cypriot flag as **Vrysi** and owned by Mavroleon's Castle Shipping Co Ltd, which had in 1970 purchased the 1937-built **Rochester Castle** which, renamed **Glenda**, was immediately resold to Chinese mainland breakers. The **Vrysi** arrived at Kaohsiung for breaking on or about 8 December 1971.

(Simon Olsen collection)

53

Liverpool's two north locks to the River Mersey, Gladstone and Langton, offer excellent close-up views of ships arriving and sailing. Ships arriving on a flood tide swing in the river to stem the tide for their approach to the lock while ships arriving on an ebb tide enter the lock stern first. Here Bank Line's **Weybank**, built at Belfast in 1964, is seen on her approach to Langton lock on the morning flood tide of 10 October 1975 on arrival from Glasgow to load for Maracaibo, Venezuela, while on charter to Harrison Line. Early in 1979 she was sold at Hong Kong to Good Harvest Marine Co. of Taiwan. Renamed **Golden Nigeria**, she arrived at Kaohsiung for breaking on 18 April 1984. Sistership **Roybank**, also sold in 1979, was wrecked at Kalilimenes, Crete, on 17 January 1985 as the Greek-owned **Byron I** during a voyage from Gdynia to India with a cargo of sugar.

(Paul Boot)

Vantage points in the River Mersey for the photography of ships calling at Liverpool, Birkenhead and Eastham, albeit at some distance, include New Brighton on the south side and Crosby on the north side. Palm Line's *Ikeja Palm*, built on Tyneside in 1961, was photographed outbound from Liverpool passing Crosby on 16 August 1981. Soon sold to the Greek-owned General Maritime Enterprises Antwerp Ltd and renamed *GME Palma*, early in 1983 she was transferred to the Greek flag and her name shortened to *Palma* as which she arrived for breaking at Gadani Beach on 24 November 1983. William Hesketh Lever, soap maker at Port Sunlight near

Bromborough, had acquired the Manchester firm of Herbert Watson & Company in 1916, renaming it Bromport Steamship, to carry raw materials such as palm kernel from West Africa. In 1923, Bromport was absorbed into Lever's Niger Company which, at around the time of Unilever's creation in 1929, merged with the African & Eastern Trade Corporation to become the United Africa Company Limited (UAC). After the war it was decided that UAC's ship owning should be separated from its other trading activities and so Palm Line was formed in 1949. In 1985 Unilever sold Palm Line to Elder Dempster Lines.

(Malcolm Cranfield)

Alfred lock entrance to Birkenhead docks offers excellent close up views of ships arriving and sailing although movements only take place on a flood tide and the Liverpool background can be a distraction. Large ships depart stern first and are swung off the entrance to head down the River Mersey when bound for sea. Here *Trefusis* of Hain-Nourse, departing from Birkenhead on 18 February 1971 fully laden bound for Khorramshahr, Iran, was turned close to the lock and photographed before the three large chimneys of the Clarence Dock power station, known as the Three Sisters, became a problem. Although the power station was demolished in 1994 new tall buildings continue to be erected in the area. *Trefusis*, built in 1961 by Readhead at South Shields for Hain S. S. Co., had in 1965 become part of the combined Hain-Nourse fleet and in 1972 became part of the P&O Group's General Cargo Division. She became *Strathteviot* in 1975, then as part of the P&O Strath Services fleet, but was sold in 1978 to Olistim Navigation, of Piraeus, and renamed *Evia*. Having arrived at Basrah from Havana on 20 August 1980, *Evia* was trapped when hostilities broke out between Iraq and Iran and subsequently abandoned. She was towed out of Basrah on 26 July 1993 as *Horizon* bound for Gadani Beach for breaking.

(Paul Boot)

As an example of a ship photographed arriving at Birkenhead, *Westbury* of Alexander Shipping Co. (Houlder Brothers) is seen off Alfred lock on 31 August 1968 on charter to a cargo liner operator to load for India. She had been swung in the river to stem the tide and was positioned to the west of the lock, slowly drifting down river before turning to port to make her approach to the lock, a difficult manoeuvre. *Westbury*, built at Burntisland in 1960 for Houlder Brothers' services to the east coast of South America or to New Zealand, had spent much time out on charter. Sold at Manchester in the autumn of 1978 to Canopus Shipping of Athens, she traded as *Diamando* for much of 1980 on charter to Cia. Nacional de Nav. of Lisbon. Late in 1980 she was sold within Greece with the continuing charter for which she was given the more appropriate name of *Polana*. When the charter ended she was sent direct from Beira to Gadani Beach for breaking, arriving there on 24 May 1983.

(Eddie Jackson, Simon Olsen collection)

Gravesend, on the south bank of the River Thames opposite Tilbury docks, has long been a favourite location for ship photography although the ships can be rather distant. In the past ships have often anchored off Gravesend, sometimes secured to buoys, while awaiting a berth. Here Palm Line's **Benin Palm**, built at Bremerhaven in 1936, is seen at anchor waiting to proceed into Tilbury docks in May 1959. Ordered from a German yard to utilise funds which could not be repatriated to the U.K., she was delivered to United Africa Co. Ltd. as **Ethiopian**, becoming **Benin Palm** in 1949. She was sold later in 1959 to the London-based Greek owner J. P. Hadoulis who renamed her **Faneromeni**. In 1961, when he sold her to Japanese breakers, he purchased sistership **Kano Palm** (ex **Guinean**), renamed **St.George** but sold in 1964, and in 1966 he bought the 1948-built **Niger Palm** (ex **Nigerian**). Renamed **Triada**, she was scrapped in 1968.

(John Mathieson, courtesy of Russell Priest - Nautical Association of Australia)

This view of Furness, Withy & Co.'s steam turbine powered **Pacific Reliance**, seen outbound from London, was taken in May 1970 from the Northfleet area of the River Thames opposite Tilbury. She was built by Vickers Armstrong in Newcastle in 1951. She was operating on Pacific Steam Navigation services to the east coast of South America but, probably for tax purposes, would be transferred to the nominal ownership of Royal Mail Lines before arriving at Bruges in Belgium for breaking on 20 April 1971. Furness, Withy & Co. was created in 1891 when the Furness Line was merged with the business of Edward Withy and Company, largely trading to New York and subsequently to the Pacific coast of the USA and Canada. Sold in 1980 to C. Y. Tung of Hong Kong, the business was resold in 1990 to Dr. Rudolf A. Oetker, operators of Hamburg South America Line which continued to serve the traditional Furness Withy trading areas until bought by Maersk at the end of 2017.

(Simon Olsen collection)

Eastham is a superb vantage point, ships using the Manchester Ship Canal passing very close to shore and often departing at speed as in the case here of Harrison Line's *Administrator*, built at the Doxford shipyard in 1958, on 4 March 1978 following a voyage from East Africa. She returned to Manchester on 26 May from Puerto Cabello, Venezuela, remaining in port until sold in the autumn. Stena Atlantic Line, which had bought her sister ship *Author*, renamed *Humber*, were to give *Administrator* the name *Tyne* but instead resold her to Oriental Maritime Pte. Ltd. of Singapore. She sailed from Manchester on 28 October 1978 as *Oriental Sea* bound for the Swedish port of Gävle (Gefle) to load for Chittagong where she arrived on 29 December 1978 and was then broken up locally. *Humber* had meanwhile arrived at Karachi on 9 November 1978 from Hamburg, suffering engine trouble en route, and was beached for breaking at Gadani Beach in June 1979.

(Paul Boot)

Photographed slowly passing Eastham inward for the locks to the Manchester Ship Canal on the mid-day tide of Saturday 22 August 1964 is Clan Line's *Clan Graham*, built at Greenock in 1962. The fifth in the fleet given that name, she was arriving from Beira in East Africa, unusually via Barrow. When sold at Mombasa in April 1981, *Clan Graham* was one of the last three ships in the Clan Line fleet, the others being *Clan Macgillivray* and *Clan Macgregor* which were sold at the end of that year. *Clan Graham* joined sister ship *Clan Grant* in a fleet managed by Navegante Shipping Agency of Hong Kong. *Clan Grant* was purchased by Navegante in 1980, trading as *Enriqueta*, while *Clan Grant* became *Mari Anne*. In mid-1983 *Mari Anne* was renamed *Candelaria* as which she arrived at Kaohsiung for breaking on 23 March 1984. Following a last loaded voyage to North Korea in November 1984 *Enriqueta* proceeded to a Chinese port in January 1985 for breaking.

(Eddie Jackson, Simon Olsen collection)

Elder Dempster Lines' **Sekondi** was built in 1948 at the Haverton Hill shipyard on Teesside. She is seen in the Manchester Ship Canal passing Ellesmere Port outbound in May 1963. She would soon moor alongside the crane berth at Eastham to prepare for sea. In 1965 she, along with five sister ships, was transferred to Guinea Gulf Line and renamed. As **Mampong**, she was sold in 1967 to the Hong Kong domiciled shipowner Quincy Chuang who renamed her **Java Sea** but sold her on in 1968 to Fortunewind Maritime Ltd, the buyers of **Ebro** (back cover) and renamed **Fortune Carrier**. She sadly sank in a typhoon off Swatow on 1 October 1968 during a voyage from Hong Kong to Hsinkang with a cargo of scrap iron. Her Furness-built sistership **Sherbro**, renamed **Matru**, was also sold in 1967, to the Greek-owned Kronos Shipping (Lemos), to trade as **Agia Eftichia** until a voyage from Safaga to Karachi where she arrived on 28 November 1971. She was then purchased by the London-based Incop Shipping Corporation (M. A. Panjwani t/a Asia Bulk Carriers Ltd) and sold to local breakers as the Somali-flagged **Moka**.

(Eddie Jackson, Simon Olsen collection)

The **Merchant** of the Charente S. S. Co. (Harrison Line) was built at the Lithgow shipyard in Port Glasgow in 1943. We see her on the Manchester Ship Canal passing Old Quay to the east of Runcorn where ships could be secured to the retaining wall to allow others sufficient space. As was the case with **Ebro** (back cover) her funnel was short enough not to require part removal for the passage. **Merchant** was a standard war-built Y6 type delivered to the British Government in April 1943 as **Empire Miranda**. Purchased by Harrison Line in 1947, she was sold in 1961 to Margalante Cia. Naviera S.A., a buyer of ships for immediate resale to breakers, using Mavroleon Brothers as London agents, which later acquired **Brisbane Star** (page 72). **Merchant** was sent to Hong Kong as **Trito** for breaking, arriving there on 26 May 1961. The Lithgow yard had built several Y-type ships between 1940 and 1945 of which Harrison Line also acquired the 1942-built Y2-type **Empire Addison**, renamed **Philosopher**, sold in 1959, and the 1943-built Y5-type **Empire Service**, renamed **Selector**, which in 1960 was also sold to breakers via Margalante.

(Eddie Jackson, courtesy of Paul Boot)

For most of the 20th century the piers at Avonmouth were very popular with ship photographers. Inward ships to Avonmouth, which until the 1950s were only photographed from the south pier, helpfully displayed two pennants in order to signal for which of the port's two locks they were bound. Both of the south and north piers offer excellent, if rather different, viewpoints at all times of the day. Ships inbound for the Royal Edward lock on a flood tide pass the north pier twice, turning up river to stem the tide for docking, while those approaching on an ebb tide take a direct approach to the lock. The *Kinnaird Castle*, the former *Clan Ross*, was built at Greenock in 1956. During 1961/2 she had operated as *South African Scientist*. She is here seen rounding the north pier inwards on the flood tide of the morning of 4 December 1970. She had departed from Mauritius on 17 October 1970 and arrived at Liverpool on 20 December. Sold late in 1975 to the Dubai-based Monnoo Overseas Ltd, which had also purchased *Argyllshire* (page 4), she traded as *Nazeer* until arriving at Gadani Beach on 26 April 1978 for breaking. Sistership *Kinpurnie Castle*, the former *Clan Stewart*, was sold to Greece in 1967 to trade as *Hellenic Med* until broken up in 1978.

(Malcolm Cranfield)

Arriving at Avonmouth later on the same tide in December 1970 was Blue Funnel Line's VC2-S-AP2 type *Myrmidon*. She was built in 1945 at Richmond, California as *Ripon Victory* and was purchased by China Mutual Steam Navigation Company Ltd. in 1947. She arrived at Kaohsiung for breaking on 27 September 1971. Several other Victory ships were purchased from the United States Maritime Commission by Blue Funnel Line as follows: *Maron*/*Rhesus* (ex *Berwyn Victory*) and *Memnon*/*Glaucus* (ex *Phillips Victory*), both sold in 1962, *Mentor* (ex *Carthage Victory*), sold in 1967, *Polyphemus*/*Tantalus* (ex *Macmurray Victory*), sold in 1969, and *Polydorus*/*Talthybius* (ex *Salina Victory*) which was also sent to Kaohsiung for breaking at the end of 1971. During the 1950s these ships were primarily employed on the Blue Sea Line service between the United States and Far East but were replaced, mainly by new "M" class ships, in the 1960s.

(Malcolm Cranfield)

Battery Point at Portishead, outside Bristol, is renowned as a marvellous location for viewing ships, which often pass at quite close quarters and at speed. The ***Anton Saefkow*** of VEB Deutsche Seereederei (DSR) is seen "passing the Point" on 25 July 1971 inbound for Avonmouth from Port Sudan. An XB-type vessel, she was built at Warnemünde in 1965. DSR's competition with the British lines had put pressure on freight rates. In an attempt to stabilize the trades, notwithstanding that the East German State was not officially recognized by the United Kingdom Government, DSR was from 1969 invited to join the liner conferences serving India and East Africa. Following two final round voyages from Rostock to Port Sudan in 1985 ***Anton Saefkow*** loaded a cargo for Da Nang in Vietnam, then proceeding to Huangpu in China for breaking, arriving on 10 December 1985. Of the sixteen X-type ships built between 1962 and 1966, two sadly soon became marine casualties while one of the four ships modified at Rijeka in the mid-1980s for the carriage of semi-finished metals from the U.S.S.R., ***Rudolf Breitscheid***, was wrecked on Klaipeda mole on 24 September 1988. DSR, formed on 1 July 1952 by the East German Communist Government, was privatised on 3 June 1993.

(Malcolm Cranfield)

Proceeding down the Bristol Channel past Portishead at speed on 24 July 1971 is the *City of Canberra* of Ellerman Lines, built in 1961 at the Barclay Curle shipyard in Glasgow. Her voyage to Avonmouth had started at Bunbury near Perth, Western Australia, on 6 April and she subsequently proceeded to load cargo at Sydney for discharge at Bordeaux and London. It is thought that she may have loaded a parcel of ore at Bunbury for discharge at Avonmouth as a final port of call. *City of Canberra* was sold in 1977 to trade as *Tasgold* for Reefer Lines Pte. Ltd. of Singapore until

arriving at Kaohsiung for breaking on 10 November 1979. Of her two sisterships built at the same yard, the 1960-built *City of Sydney*, renamed *City of Montreal* in 1971, was also "sold East" in 1977 and, as *Yat Fei*, broken up in 1979, while the 1964-built *City of Adelaide*, renamed *City of Canterbury* in 1973, was sold to Belgium in 1975 to trade as *Rubens* until laid up at Antwerp in March 1982. In June 1983 she sailed as *A. L. Pioneer* bound for Chittagong where she was soon beached for breaking.

(Malcolm Cranfield)

Cardiff docks were very popular with ship photographers during the 20th century. The docks had open areas of quayside, interesting working berths and accessible piers from which to photograph ships in the morning, from the east side, and in the evening from the west side. In addition Penarth Head, seen in the background to this photograph, gave opportunities for photography from both high and low levels. Cardiff Bay Barrage now provides a similar low level view. Here the **Emilia Plater** of Polish Ocean Lines is seen from the west pier arriving at Cardiff on the evening of 24 April 1975 during a voyage from Sydney to Gdynia. Built at Gdansk in 1959, **Emilia Plater** was one of eleven of the B54 type built for Poland between 1956 and 1962 while nine were built for the U.S.S.R. and six for other flags. She arrived at Shanghai for breaking on 21 December 1984. The tug **Danegarth** was built at Lowestoft in 1966 for R. & J. H. Rea. Owned by Cory Towage at the time of this photograph, she was sold to Greece in 1992 and remains in operation as **Linoperamata**.

(Nigel Jones)

Custom House Quay, Greenock, the location of this photograph of Blue Funnel Line's *Anchises* outbound from Glasgow, is a superb vantage point on the River Clyde. Built at Dundee in 1947, *Anchises* became famous in June 1949 when attacked near Shanghai by Chinese Nationalist fighter bombers. Her engine room was flooded and she settled by the stern in shallow water but was subsequently refloated and towed to Kobe for repairs. In August 1972 she was at Rotterdam, reportedly to be renamed *Asphalion* but instead sailed for the Far East, still as *Anchises*. The name

Asphalion was instead allocated to sister ship *Polyphemus* in November 1972. By January 1973 *Anchises* was renamed *Alcinous*, sailing from Swansea for the Far East owned by China Mutual S. N. (CMSN). Then, in August 1974, she was transferred to Glen Line for a single voyage from Middlesbrough to Bangkok and back before returning to CMSN ownership. *Alcinous* (ex *Anchises*) was sold for breaking in 1975, arriving at Kaohsiung on 5 September 1975.

(Trevor Jones collection)

In addition to its well known piers, the River Tyne has several good vantage points for ship photography. The **Patani** of Elder Dempster Lines was built at Greenock in 1954. She is here seen on 19 September 1964 from the shore at Felling, an eastern suburb of Gateshead, midway between the major Tyneside shipbuilding and repair yards and Newcastle Quay where her cargo will be discharged. She is seen inbound during a voyage from Lobito to London via Newcastle. Soon afterwards her funnel was heightened to allow improved smoke dispersal. Sister ship **Perang** was soon to be towed from London to Sunderland, arriving there on 18 October, the same work probably having been done there. **Patani** was sold in November 1972 to Mitchurst Ltd, owned by the Shaikh family, of London, then trading east of Suez as **Patwari** until arriving for breaking at Gadani Beach on 24 January 1978. The same buyers had between 1975 and 1978 operated the former **Roland/Dunedin Star**, renamed **Jessica**, and the former **Clan MacLeod**, renamed **Papaji**.

(Malcolm Donnelly)

The Nieuwe Waterweg (New Waterway) has always been popular with ship photographers, the most favoured locations being Hoek van Holland, Maassluis and particularly Rozenburg on the south bank. Over the decades the background at each location has much changed, for example with woods growing opposite Rozenburg. Since the late 1960s the steady building of new docks at Europoort and Maasvlakte has greatly reduced the volume of shipping passing those old favourite spots. Here

Blue Funnel Line's **Clytoneus**, built at Dundee in 1948, is seen passing Rozenburg, outbound from Rotterdam, in July 1971. She arrived at Kaohsiung for breaking on 20 June 1972. Unlike many of her sister ships, although in common with **Anchises** (page 67), she was always employed in Ocean's Blue Funnel Line services to the Far East and not transferred in later years to Elder Dempster services.

(Simon Olsen collection)

Seen in the Nieuwe Waterweg inward for Rotterdam passing Maassluis during July 1966 is **Sarpedon** owned by Koninklijke Nederlandsche Stoomboot Mij (K.N.S.M.) and a Hansa A type ship built at Bolnes in 1947. Ordered by the German Government during the war for operation by Oldenburg-Portugiesische Dampfs. Rhederei (OPDR) as **Saturn**, it had been decided to complete the ship as **Sperrbrecher 31**, but in May 1945 the ship was still building and declared a spoil of war. Purchased by K.N.S.M. on 25 January 1946, it is understood the ship was originally to be named **Periander** but instead launched as **Sarpedon**. Sold to Greece in July 1968, she sailed from Rotterdam as **Agia Skepi** for Canton (now Guangzhou) and never returned to Europe. Sold to Far East buyers in 1971, latterly as **Cheng Lung**, she capsized and sank on 25 July 1977 following a collision at Kaohsiung during typhoon Thelma. Refloated on 17 April 1978, she was soon broken up locally. The Amsterdam-based K.N.S.M. (Royal Netherlands Steamship Company), once the largest company in Amsterdam and one of the top five shipping lines in the Netherlands, had existed from 1856 to 1981 when it merged with Nedlloyd.

(Simon Olsen collection)

The River Scheldt, linking Antwerp to the North Sea, has several well known vantage points for ship photography including the Dutch towns of Vlissingen (Flushing) on the north bank and Terneuzen and Walsoorden on the south bank. Although flying a Belgian courtesy flag, it is thought that this May 1975 photograph of DDG Hansa's *Axenfels*, built at Bremen in 1958, was taken from the old ferry pier at Walsoorden outbound from Antwerp in the late afternoon; she arrived at Hamburg on 17 May 1975 from Calcutta. Unusually, until 1969, *Axenfels* was technically managed on behalf of DDG Hansa by Ahlers N.V. of Antwerp, which had operated her as *Schelde*. In March 1972 she was chartered to the newly-created Royal Nepal Shipping Co. of Kathmandu as *Narenda Laxmi* as part of a cooperation agreement which was terminated in April 1972. Sold in 1977 to Naphtec Inspektions of Hamburg, she operated as *Sternal Trader* until resold in 1981 to A. G. Politis, of Piraeus. Renamed *Socrates*, she was laid up at Ithaka from 4 July 1982 until sailing for Gadani Beach late in 1986 for breaking. DDG Hansa, founded at Bremen in 1881, became a specialist in heavy lifts, in particular serving Persian Gulf ports, but declared bankruptcy in 1980.

(Karl-Josef Hagenkötter collection)

Along the River Elbe in Germany there are numerous fine places from which to view ships including Cuxhaven and Brunsbüttel towards the mouth of the river and Wedel and Blankenese on the east bank near Hamburg. Blue Star Line's historic *Brisbane Star*, built by Cammell Laird in 1937, is here seen passing Blankenese, outbound from Hamburg on 7 July 1955 during a voyage from Hobart to Hamburg, Hull and London. On 31 July 1942 *Brisbane Star* entered the Firth of Clyde, where she and her sister *Melbourne Star* joined the Convoy WS 21S for Operation Pedestal to relieve the siege of Malta. On 12 August, off Cap Bona, Luftwaffe aircraft launched an aerial torpedo at her, severely damaging her bow, but she stayed afloat. Anchoring off Sousse in the Gulf of Hammamet, Vichy French Tunisia, the harbour master ordered her to be detained and enter port but her master, Captain Frederick Riley, refused and later proceeded, escorted by Spitfires, the 200 miles to Valletta, where she safely reached the Grand Harbour on 14 August 1942. *Melbourne Star* was very sadly lost with 113 lives on 2 April 1943 when torpedoed by U-129 during a voyage from Liverpool to Australia with a cargo of stores and munitions; there were just four survivors. *Brisbane Star* was sold in August 1963 and renamed *Enea* for a single voyage from Rotterdam and Hamburg to Hong Kong before proceeding to Izumiōtsu near Osaka in Japan for breaking, arriving there on 15 October 1963.

(Herbert Voss, courtesy of Gerhard Fiebiger)

The 16-knot *Pasadena* of the Danish East Asiatic Company (EAC) was built at Hamburg in 1953. She is seen at speed in the River Elbe in June 1969. She subsequently sailed from Copenhagen for Middlesbrough to complete loading for the Far East, returning from Saigon in September 1969. In mid-1972 she was sold to Hong Kong Islands Shipping Co. to trade as *Tungku Chau* until arriving at Kaohsiung for breaking on 10 April 1979. EAC was founded in the spring of 1897 by H. N. Andersen, a Danish expatriate with a large network in Asia, starting a service between Copenhagen and Bangkok. In its prime, in addition to a shipping line, EAC was a global conglomerate spanning shipbuilding, slaughterhouses, plantations, pharmaceuticals and other industries. Its business peaking in 1970, EAC's fortunes rapidly declined with the shipping line's last vessel, the 1996-built bulk carrier *Selandia* being sold in 2013.

(Simon Olsen collection)

The Kiel Canal in northern Germany has long been regarded as a haven for ship photography. From Brunsbüttel locks at the River Elbe end to Kiel Holtenau locks at the Baltic end, and at many points in between, there are excellent accessible vantage points to view ships at close quarters. Photographed mid-canal near Rendsburg on 3 July 1976 during a voyage from Ipswich to Gdynia was **Baltic Arrow** of the United Baltic Corporation (UBC), built at Hamburg in 1956. UBC, formed in 1919, was until 1982 an equal partnership between Andrew Weir and the East Asiatic Company of Copenhagen. In 1974, following the crash of a Turkish Airlines flight on takeoff from Paris to London with the deputy General Manager of UBC on board, the management of UBC was integrated with that of MacAndrews & Company Ltd., a long established business which became part of Andrew Weir Shipping in 1935. The joint business was sold to CMA CGM on 31 December 2002 and, following its acquisition of OPDR, is now managed from Hamburg. Having been sold in mid-1978, **Baltic Arrow** sadly foundered as the Costa Rica owned **Sea Pacific** on 16 December 1983 during a voyage from Callao to Corinto with a cargo of zinc bars and steel coils.

(Jan-Erik Andersson, courtesy of Douglas Cromby)

In the final section of our book, we look at tramp ships. Power Steamship Company Ltd's Burntisland-built *Huntsmore* is seen in the River Thames passing London's Royal Docks inbound for an upriver dock. Delivered to McCowen & Gross Ltd on 20 May 1951 as *Derrymore*, by the end of the year Donald McCowan withdrew from the partnership giving Oscar Gross & Sons Ltd sole control of Power Steamship and she was renamed. The 1943-built *Derrynane* was similarly renamed *Huntsbrook* while their three other ships were sold. On 3 October 1966, during a voyage from New Westminster to Avonmouth, Liverpool and Manchester, *Huntsmore* was disabled by generator trouble and in April 1967,

while on voyage from Santiago to Trieste, she suffered a crankcase explosion off the Azores. Towed into São Miguel by *Huntsland*, which was nearby on a voyage from Fiji to the U.K., *Huntsmore* was then towed to her destination by the tug *Nisos Kerkyra*. Soon repaired, she returned to Cuba only to suffer a collision on the return voyage to Europe necessitating a tow into Rotterdam by the tug *Thames*, arriving on 10 December 1967. Having already been sold to Papalios of Greece, she was repaired and resumed trading with Cuba as *Aegis Hope* until sailing from Casablanca in September 1973 for Shanghai where she was broken up.

(Malcolm Cranfield collection)

Trafalgar S. S. Co. Ltd.'s **Newhill**, built at Dumbarton in 1943, is seen sailing from London on 20 July 1965 bound for Cuba, the photo location being in the region of Tilbury landing stage opposite Northfleet. **Newhill**, operated by the London-based Greek-owned Tsavliris Shipping Ltd, was built as **Pegu** for British & Burmese S. N.Co. Ltd. but purchased in 1950 by Ben Line Steamers Ltd, of Leith. Renamed **Benattow**, her port of registry of Leith was retained when sold to Tsavliris in 1963. Similarly the Cardiff registry was retained on purchase by Tsavliris of **Restormel** in 1964, which as **Newglade** was nominally owned by Waterloo Shipping Ltd. **Newhill** had survived a grounding at the entrance of Santiago harbour in Cuba in March 1964 and was laid up at Piraeus on 9 August 1966 and arrived at Castellon in Spain on 11 November 1967 for breaking.

(Malcolm Cranfield collection)

The Gibraltar-registered **St. Joanna**, formerly **Cape York** of Lyle Shipping, was built at the Lithgow shipyard in Port Glasgow, in 1955. She is seen passing Gravesend, inbound for Tilbury Dock from India in March 1967 while on charter to Ellerman City Liners. A dock pilot has boarded and Port of London health officials wait to board her and carry out necessary formalities. Her tugs are already secured ahead of swinging her in the river to approach the lock. **St. Joanna** had been purchased by Greek interests, thought to be Despina Rodopoulos and Alexander Skoutaris, in September 1965. After completing discharge of her cargo at Dundee, she sailed for Piraeus to be renamed **Alexandros S.**, bearing unchanged funnel colours until at least May 1970. She became **Alexandros Skoutaris** at Bombay in December 1971 and at some point given new funnel colours incorporating the letters R and S. Sold in January 1979 to Far East interests as **Primo Arabia**, she undertook only one voyage before lying idle at Singapore for a year from March 1979 until sent to Kaohsiung for breaking.

(Ken Wightman - Malcolm Cranfield collection)

St. Essylt was built in 1948 for South American Saint Line, of Cardiff, by J. L. Thompson, Sunderland. She was photographed from a vantage point opposite Tilbury Docks at Rosherville, Gravesend, outbound from London. It is thought that this was on a voyage from Rosario to London and Hamburg, a trade on which she was often employed, possibly on her last voyage in May 1965. In July 1965 she loaded a cargo at Casablanca for Shanghai at the start of a new career in the Far East, serving the South Pacific islands and New Zealand as China Navigation's **Yunnan**. Early in 1971 she was sold to Prosperity Steamship of Hong Kong to trade as **Lucky Two** until arriving at Kaohsiung on 23 January 1979 for breaking. South American Saint Line had started out in 1926 as Barry Shipping Co, its ships mostly engaged as tramps but also heavily involved in the coal trade to Buenos Aires, returning with cargoes of grain, for which service the company was renamed South American Saint Line in 1936. The company lost twelve vessels during the Second World War and in 1945 ordered two new passenger/cargo liners, delivered as **St. Essylt** and **St. Thomas**. In 1965 the service was taken over by Houlder Brothers.

(Malcolm Cranfield collection)

Susan Constant was photographed on the River Mersey, inbound for Ellesmere Port from Hampton Roads, on 18 May 1971. Built by J. Samuel White at East Cowes in 1958, she was renamed ***Marson Cathy*** at Cardiff in March 1973 before being sold on in 1974 to Nigeria and in 1981 to Chile where she was broken up in 1989 as ***Chiloe IV***. The Constant family of Gravesend had opened an office in Cardiff in 1929 but in 1973 sold out to Dovey Shipping & Industrial Holdings.

(Paul Boot)

Houlder Line Ltd's **St. Merriel** was built by Bartram, Sunderland, in 1954. She is seen at Birkenhead on 5 July 1970 discharging a cargo of grain from Rosario. Built as **Thorpe Grange**, her name was changed in 1966 after Houlder had acquired the trading rights of South American Saint Line. In September 1971 she reverted to **Thorpe Grange** but, after discharging another cargo of grain at Birkenhead, she was sent to Falmouth. Laid up there from 23 November 1971 until August 1972, **Thorpe Grange** then proceeded to Swansea and Glasgow to load for Buenos Aires. On returning to Glasgow in December 1972 her name reverted to **St. Merriel** but one year later she was sold to Singapore interests to trade as **Joo Hong**. Early in 1975 she was sold to Li-Ta Shipping and by the end of 1975 renamed **Pan Teck**, then one

year later **Liva**. However after arriving at Colombo on 25 March 1977 **Liva** broke her moorings, suffering a collision, and on 19 March 1979 left under tow of the tug **Orinoco** bound for Kaohsiung for breaking. Houlder Brothers & Co. was formed in London in 1856 and in 1881 entered the River Plate passenger and cargo trade. In 1911 Furness, Withy & Co. purchased a 50% stake in Houlder Bros and withdrew from the Federal - Houlder - Shire partnership. A substantial holding in Alexander Shipping Co. was purchased in 1937 and complete control was achieved in 1947. In 1980 the remaining Houlder Line ships were transferred to Furness, Withy (Shipping) Ltd.

(Paul Boot)

Chapman & Willan's *Lynton* was built in 1957 by Short Bros, Sunderland. She is seen approaching Eastham on 9 July 1972 already partly prepared for the transit up the Manchester Ship Canal at the end of her last voyage thus named, with a cargo of grain from East London, South Africa. She subsequently sailed from Manchester in September 1972 as *Five Star*, owned by Abbas Gokal's Gulf Shipping Group. It seems that she was renamed *Five Stars* at Piraeus in April 1977 before being sold for breaking at Gadani Beach where she arrived on 20 August 1979. Ralph Chapman and Thomas R. Miller had formed a partnership in 1878 which led to the formation of R. Chapman & Son in 1896, tramp ship operators, which became Chapman & Willan in 1951. In 1967 a new bulk carrier named *Demeterton* was built for the company at South Shields but in 1974, together with the 1968-built *Frumenton*, she was transferred to Burnett Steamship which, then owned by Fednav of Canada, had purchased the company.

(Paul Boot)

Hogarth's **Baron Jedburgh** was built in 1958 at the Readhead shipyard in South Shields. She was photographed at Avonmouth at the end of March 1967 waiting for West Wharf 5 berth ahead of her to be vacated in order to start discharge of a cargo of ore concentrate from Mackay, Queensland, Australia. Her last voyage started in August 1967 from nearby Mourilyan to the UK with a cargo of sugar. Then sold to Atlantic Shipping (N. Tsimplis) of Piraeus, she traded for ten years as **Evie G. Chimples** until returning to Piraeus on 9 June 1977 where she was renamed **Global Mariner** under the ownership of Lelakis Shipping. Sadly she ran aground on 30 December 1978 during a voyage from Nantes to Assab with a cargo of bagged wheat and was towed to Massawa anchorage before having to be beached and presumably broken up "in situ". Hugh Hogarth & Sons, Glasgow, were tramp ship owners from 1881 and had joined forces in 1968 with Lyle Shipping to create Scottish Ship Management. Hogarth's last ship, launched in Japan in 1983 as **Baron Dunmore**, was completed in 1985 as **Bergen Maru** because Hogarth had ceased business.

(Richard Parsons, courtesy of John D Hill)

Following overnight snow, Saturday 14 February 1970 was a brilliant, clear day on the Bristol Channel and, as Avonmouth's Royal Edward lock had been under repair for several days, the midday tide was extremely busy with Metcalfe Shipping Company's *Fidentia* the last ship to dock on the ebb tide. She was built at the shipyard of Wm Doxford in Sunderland in 1956. The visibility was so good that Newport's power station can be seen in the distance behind the ship. John Metcalfe had started Metcalfe Shipping Company at West Hartlepool in 1929 with the purchase of a new ship named *Dunelmia* from the local builder Wm. Gray. Following his death in 1971 his sons Thomas and John Ovington Metcalfe assumed control, soon selling *Fidentia*, the former *Kepwickhall* purchased in 1966 from West Hartlepool S.N. Co., and taking delivery of two new SD14s named *Dunelmia* and *Industria*. In September 1979 the company was sold to Furness Withy together with its remaining ship, a newly-built SD14 named *Dunelmia*, delivered in July 1977. *Fidentia*, purchased by Maldives Shipping and renamed *Premier Arctic*, was beached for breaking at Gadani Beach, Pakistan, on 30 May 1979.

(Peter Fitzpatrick collection)

The **Marylyn** was operated by Walmar S. S. Co. (Kaye, Son & Co). She was built in 1953 at the Readhead yard in South Shields. She was photographed on 31 March 1962 when laid up between Dunston and Elswick on the River Tyne. This quiet spot, some two miles upstream from Newcastle Quay, was the uppermost navigable limit on the River Tyne for a vessel of that size. She spent some weeks laid up there during the world recession at the time but resumed trading until sold in the autumn of 1965 to clients of K&M Shipbrokers, of London. Renamed **Ionic Sky**, early in 1967 she was further renamed **Kaanthos** and placed under the management of the New York-based Anthony Culucundis. In September 1968, during a voyage from Antwerp to Colombo, she suffered boiler trouble, having to be towed into Pointe Noire, returning to Rotterdam in May 1969. Towed by **Fairplay XI**, she left Rotterdam on 30 September 1969 to Bilbao for repairs following a sale to other New York-based

Greek owners. As **Antinous** she ran aground near Genoa in March 1970 but, after repairs lasting several months, she resumed trading worldwide until sold in the Far East during March 1971 to the New York-based World Tide Shipping Corporation. As **Ocean Glory** she foundered on 4 July 1971 during a voyage from Bandar Shahpour to Visakhapatnam with a cargo of sulphur, her crew being saved by British India's **Chilka**. The origins of Kaye, Son & Co. may be traced back to 1893 when Frederick Kaye left Houlder Brothers, purchasing his first ship in 1912. The "K" Steamship Co. Ltd was formed in 1919 and in 1926 four new ships were financed by a partnership between Kaye, Son and Co. Ltd. and the Lithgow shipyard in the form of the jointly owned Walmar Steamship Co. Ltd. During 1973, Kaye, Son and Co. Ltd. was absorbed into the Furness, Withy Group.

(Malcolm Donnelly)

The *Frank Leonhardt*, owned by Leonhardt & Blumberg of Hamburg, was built at Flensburg in 1955. She was photographed outbound from Rotterdam in July 1971 at a time when she was regularly loading a cargo, possibly fishmeal, at Egersund in Norway for Genoa with an occasional call at Rotterdam on the return leg. Leonhardt & Blumberg, which started business in 1903, had lost all its ships during the Second World War and started to rebuild its fleet in 1950 with the acquisition of the 1924-built *Miguel de Larrinaga*, renamed *Bernd Leonhardt*. She was sold in 1954 to help finance a newbuilding programme of four identical ships including *Frank Leonhardt* and the company has since been highly successful, in 2017 creating Leonhardt & Blumberg Ship Management as a partner to Hanseatic Unity chartering. *Frank Leonhardt* was sold to China in 1972, trading as *White Sea* under Yick Fung Shipping & Enterprises management until beached for breaking at Bombay on 16 March 1983.

(Simon Olsen collection)

The Italian-owned *Jolanda* is seen from a position opposite Hoek van Holland inbound for Rotterdam in July 1970. She was built in 1940 at the Lithgow shipyard in Port Glasgow as *Ribera* for the Bolton Steam Shipping Company (Bolton S. S.). She had become the Goulandris-owned *Okeanis* in 1955 and was purchased in 1959 by Societa Armamento Marittimo (SOARMA) of Genoa which, like Bolton S. S., had painted its ships' funnels plain black. *Jolanda* arrived for breaking at Sveti Kajo, near Split in Croatia, on 10 June 1971. Bolton S. S., formed in London in 1885, had operated tramp ships and, from 1956, iron ore carriers until taking delivery in 1965 of the bulk carrier *Ribera*. She was sold in 1973 and replaced with two new bulkers named *Reynolds* and *Rubens* on the funnels of which were painted a red band and the company's house flag. These ships were transferred in 1982 to Nosira Shipping, a company formed by Ted Arison, the creator of Carnival Cruise Lines, with Bolton Maritime Management Ltd as manager until the ships were sold in the late 1980s.

(Peter Fitzpatrick collection)

The **Silksworth** was the first bulk carrier to be owned by Watergate S. S. Co. (R. S. Dalgliesh & Co), of Newcastle). She was built in 1964 by J. L. Thompson, Sunderland, She was photographed at Rotterdam in July 1971 following a voyage from Port-Cartier in Quebec, probably with a cargo of iron ore. Arriving on the Tyne on 10 September 1972 for repairs following a grounding, there she was sold to China. As **China Sea** and managed by Yick Fung Shipping & Enterprises of Hong Kong, she sailed on 2 December 1972 for Romania to load her first cargo to Hsinkang, now Tianjin. In 1976 her registration was moved to Qingdao and her name changed to **Hua Hai**, managed by China Ocean Shipping. Her last international voyage was to Tacoma in June 1987 and she was reportedly broken up in 1994. Dalgliesh Steam Shipping Co was formed in Newcastle in 1906. Seven ships were lost during the Second World War and by 1979 the last of their ships, **Naworth**, was sold and the company went into liquidation.

(Simon Olsen collection)

The **Amstelmeer**, owned by N.V. Rederij "Amsterdam", was built at Capelle aan den IJssel in 1956. She was photographed sailing from Vancouver in October 1965 on a return voyage to China. She was a true tramp ship, having sailed from La Pallice on 30 April for China and from Iquique on 15 August for Tsingtao. In 1969 she was sold to Franco Shipping of Athens to trade as **Elpida** until arriving at Bombay on 29 December 1981 and was then broken up. N.V. Rederij "Amsterdam" commenced trading in 1946 with **Amstelstad**, the former **Ocean Merchant** dating from 1942. She was sold in 1959 to China, a nation with which the company often traded, lasting until the end of the 1970s. **Amstelmeer** was the company's second newbuilding, the first being **Amstelkroon** in 1952. In 1970 N.V. Rederij "Amsterdam" became part of the newly-created consortium Holland Bulk Transport which became part of Nedlloyd in 1977.

(Ken Brodie, Harry Stott collection)

This is a fine image of *La Hacienda*, the former *Francois L. D.*, in the St. Lawrence Seaway bound from Chicago to Genoa in the spring of 1964. The photo was taken from the Jacques Cartier bridge, about ¾ of a mile from the seaway entrance. In the background is Île Sainte-Hélène (Saint Helen's Island), in the early stages of development for Expo 67, and behind that the galleries used to transport grain on conveyor belts to elevators. *La Hacienda*, built at St. Nazaire in 1953 for Louis Dreyfus & Cie, had in 1961 been transferred to Buries, Markes to replace a ship of the same name which had been sold in 1960 to Nigeria to become *Oranyan*. Retaining her British registry when sold in 1965 to Cie. Maritime et Commercial of Paris, a company linked with Argentina's Independent Plate Line, the *La Hacienda* traded as *Valparaiso* until 1971, then as *Mombasa*, before being sold to Greece in 1974 to become *Perla*. Briefly trading in 1981/82 for the Al Shirawi Group of Dubai as *Intra Sand*, she was beached for breaking at Bombay in March 1982. Buries, Markes Ltd was created in 1930 by shipbroker Howard Houlder but became dormant from 1934 until its acquisition in 1937 by the French company Louis Dreyfus. Entering the bulk ore trade in 1958, Buries, Markes joined with Mowinckels and Jebsen of Norway in 1969 to form the Gearbulk consortium while also taking delivery of its first coastal oil tankers.

(Harry Stott)

Bowater Steamship Company's **Phyllis Bowater** was built at Dumbarton in 1960. We see her at Montréal in the summer of 1968 approaching the turn for the entrance to the St. Lawrence Seaway leading into the Great Lakes. The founder of the Bowater paper making business was William Vansittart Bowater (1838-1907). His grandson, Eric Vansittart Bowater, had in 1926 opened a new mill at Northfleet on the Thames, at a location well placed for the import of Scandinavian or Canadian woodpulp. A 1954 review of Bowater's business led to the building of six small ships, of which **Phyllis Bowater** was the fifth, suitable for the pulp trade from Scandinavia to the UK and also for the Newfoundland and Tennessee mills. Bowater Steamship itself was created in February 1955 by the Bowater Corporation to operate its own ships, initially managed by Furness Withy and later by British & Commonwealth. Unusual was the fleet's paint scheme of Brunswick green with a light green boot topping (later replaced by red oxide) and cream upper works. On 12 January 1973 **Phyllis Bowater** departed from the Tyne as **Charlotte**, owned by Dimitrios Carapanos of Piraeus, trading worldwide until the autumn of 1978 when resold to J. G. Kapranis who renamed her **Tassos K**. For much of 1982 she was trading out of Samsun, Turkey, from mid-year under the new name of **Malero M. I.** before proceeding to Malta where she was sold to Marti Shipping & Trading of Istanbul, sailing on 26 February 1983 as **Naz K**. Following an October 1988 call into the Mersey from India she was purchased by Ziya Kalkavan, continuing to trade as **Naz K**. until departing from Izmir in January 2001 for Kandla, and then to Alang for breaking, making her the longest surviving Bowater ship.

(Harry Stott)

Counties Ship Management's 1944-built **Denmark Hill**, the former **Fort Mattagami**, is seen arriving at Montréal on 16 October 1966 from Pangnirtung on Baffin Island. It is understood that the Canadian Government's annual summer re-supply of its northern outposts could if necessary be carried out by chartered Commonwealth ships, i.e. British ships such as **Denmark Hill**. It involved the employment of heavy barges for beach unloading. By December 1966 she was on voyage from Gdynia to Chittagong. Following a voyage at the end of 1967 from Jacksonville to India, she arrived at Kaohsiung for breaking on 23 February 1968 from Karwar in north-west India. Manuel Kulukundis, who moved from Greece to London in 1920, had together with his cousin Minas Rethymnis, soon founded the Rethymnis & Kulukundis (R&K) shipbroking business and established Counties Ship Management in 1936. **Denmark Hill** was Counties' last wartime standard cargo ship and their last managed ships were the 1970-built **County Clare** and **Helene**, both sold in 1974. Fourteen standard war built ships were purchased between 1945 and 1950 to make a total of eighteen ships operated during much of the 1950s with the number steadily reducing during the 1960s.

(Harry Stott)

The **Richard de Larrinaga** was built in 1955 at the shipyard of Wm. Pickersgill in Sunderland. She is seen arriving at Durban for bunkers in early 1970 during a voyage from the Far East. By April 1970 she had been sold to Halcoussis of Greece and, renamed **Adamandios**, was at Recife loading a cargo of sugar for Marseille. By the end of 1973 she had been resold in the Far East to Shun Fong Maritime of Taiwan and renamed **Fong Min**. Unfortunately she suffered a fire on 27 May 1975 and was condemned for breaking. The origins of the Larrinaga Steamship Company go back to Olano y Cia of Bilbao who had operated services from Liverpool to the Philippines and Cuba from the 1860s. In 1883 the Olano family sold out to the Larrinaga family and in 1898 a new company, Miguel de Larrinaga Steamship Company was registered in Liverpool. The two companies merged in 1931 to form the Larrinaga Steamship Company Ltd. Rising oil prices and political considerations caused the sale of the company in 1974 to George Vergottis who renamed it Vergocean Steamship Company Ltd. Larrinaga's last three ships were SD14s, two of which remained in the fleet when purchased by Vergottis.

(Ken Fletcher, Trevor Jones collection)

Avenue Shipping Company's **Donegal** is seen sailing from Durban in February 1974 following a call for bunkers during a return voyage from Calcutta to the U.K. and Rotterdam while on charter to Clan Line. She had sailed outwards from the Tees in September 1973 bound for Bombay and Calcutta. She was built in 1957 at the shipyard of Alexander Stephen & Sons at Linthouse on the River Clyde. From 1972 she was managed by the P&O Group's General Cargo Division and in 1975 was renamed **Strathirvine** as part of the P&O Strath Services fleet. She was sold in 1977 and renamed **Athina**, being managed on behalf of Maldives Shipping by the UAE-based Zenith Management Corporation. She arrived at Kaohsiung for breaking on 25 May 1980. The London-based shipping agents Birt, Potter & Hughes had established the Avenue Shipping Company as their shipowning division in 1924, the name being derived from their office address at 2 Fenchurch Avenue. Allan Hughes had been a major shareholder in Federal Steam Navigation on its takeover by the New Zealand Shipping Company in 1912 and this link was developed in 1954 when the Avenue Shipping Company, dormant since 1934, was reactivated. Four small part-refrigerated ships, displaced by new ships on the New Zealand to East Coast North America trade, were then transferred to Avenue ownership but independently managed by Trinder, Anderson & Company. When not employed on New Zealand Shipping Company's cargo liner services these four ships plus the **Enton**, transferred from Birt, Potter & Hughes and renamed **Limerick**, were chartered out.

(Trevor Jones)

Reardon Smith's **Devon City**, built in 1960 at the Wm. Doxford yard in Sunderland, sails from Durban early in April 1970 following a call for bunkers during a voyage from Newcastle (NSW) to Hamburg. On 17 March 1972 she arrived on the River Tyne to be handed over to clients of the London Greek Pergamos Shipping (A. K. Antoniou) and renamed **Executive Venture**. On 17 February 1973 she arrived at Singapore with engine damage and eventually sailed from Port Kelang on 14 May bound for Ashtabula on the Great Lakes but arrived at Cape Town in tow on 8 June. Again repaired, following discharge of her cargo in November 1973, she was sold to Kie Hock of Singapore, joining sister ship **Orient City** which, as **Alexander A. S.**, had been purchased from clients of the same Greek manager. Renamed **Tong Beng**,

in 1978 her management was transferred to a new company, Ban Hock, and her name changed to **Penta Y**. She arrived for breaking at Kaohsiung on 25 April 1986, two years after her sister. After an early seagoing career, in 1905 William Reardon Smith from Appledore founded his own shipping company, based in Cardiff, initially to participate in the South Wales coal trade to South America, returning with grain, but growing into a worldwide tramp and cargo liner operator. Acquiring several new bulk carriers between 1964 and 1977, the company continued to prosper and in 1972 contracted ship management for Transportación Marítima Mexicana (TMM) but by 1985 had ceased trading due to the poor prospects in the industry.

(Ken Fletcher, Trevor Jones collection)

No book of this type would be complete without an SD14. **London Cavalier**, built in 1972 by Austin & Pickersgill, Sunderland, was laid down as **London Halberdier**. She was photographed arriving at Cape Town on 6 March 1978 during a voyage from the Far East to Nigeria. She subsequently sailed from Lagos on 17 August 1978 and was sold towards the end of 1979 to clients of Vroon's Handels & Scheepvaart of Breskens. Placed under the Philippines flag and renamed **Asian Liner**, less than one year later she was sold to Componave of Portugal and renamed **Silaga**. Finally she was purchased in 1987 by An. G. Politis of Piraeus who traded her as **Socrates** until beached for breaking at Alang on 11 June 2001. London & Overseas Freighters, created in 1949 by Rethymnis & Kulukundis, had initially operated ten dry cargo ships, all transferred from Counties Ship Management Ltd. London & Overseas had started to modernise its dry cargo fleet in 1972 with four SD14s which were followed in 1977 by three B26 type bulk carriers, all of which were sold by 1983, the company thereafter operating only a small number of tankers until being sold in 1997 to the Swedish company Frontline Shipping A/B.

(Ian Shiffman, Malcolm Cranfield collection)

Rowland & Marwood (Headlam of Whitby) had purchased the **Sandsend** in 1947. She was an EC2-S-C1 type Liberty ship built in Baltimore in 1944 as **Samindoro**. We see her departing from Cape Town. She subsequently sailed from Durban on 10 August 1967 bound for China, arriving at Kaohsiung for breaking on 5 December 1967. William Headlam, who had gained initial experience in the 1880s with Robinson & Rowland of Whitby, and from 1915 was in business with Lewis G. Rowland as Headlam & Rowland, went on to head the Rowland & Marwood's S. S. Company Ltd. and in 1929 created Headlam & Sons S. S. Company Ltd. Rowland & Marwood had owned a succession of tramp ships, concluding with the 1962-built **Egton**, whose chequered career concluded with almost nine years laid up at Hartlepool until 6 January 1986 before being broken up in Finland.

(Ken Fletcher, Trevor Jones collection)

The **Appledore**, seen at Manila on 11 August 1963, was registered in London and nominally owned by Maritime Shipping & Trading Co. but in fact beneficially Greek owned by Michalinos & Co. Ltd. Built at West Hartlepool in 1953, she subsequently sailed from Geraldton in Western Australia on 12 September 1963 bound for London. Michalinos Tachmindji had created Michalinos Maritime in Piraeus in 1889 and started business in London in 1893. In 1951 the company was purchased outright by John A. Tachmindji who had in 1942 acquired from Mr. G. C. Gibson, nephew of Lord Glanely, the Bideford-registered Maritime Shipping & Trading Co. together with their 1929-built ship **Appledore** which was sold in 1951. Her pictured replacement was sold in mid-1964 to Persian Shipping Services (London) Ltd and renamed **Persian Roxana**. At Copenhagen in March 1965, she was handed over to Frangos Bros. of Greece to trade as **Marigo F.** until arriving at Bombay on 28 December 1970 where she was to be sold to Jebshun Shipping of Hong Kong and renamed **Precious Gem**. However the sale fell through and in September 1971 she was laid up at Singapore, departing under tow of the tug **Tasman Zee** on 1 March 1972 bound for Hong Kong and from there on to Whampoa intended for breaking, arriving on 19 March. Nonetheless she could have continued trading locally around China.

(George Wilson)